aircraft illustrated
ANNUAL 1985

£4.95

Cover:
British Airways Concorde, the last 'Bristol' aeroplane to be produced, received its UK certificate of airworthiness 10 years ago on 5 December 1975 and entered service on the trans-Atlantic route on 21 January 1976.

Below:
Tornado GR1s of the Tri-National Tornado Training Establishment at Cottesmore display their tail code markings which identify two from the RAF and one Luftwaffe aircraft. *Sgt B. Lawrence, RAF*

aircraft illustrated ANNUAL 1985

Edited by Peter R. March

LONDON

IAN ALLAN LTD

Right:

Sinister shape of the Lockheed SR-71 'Blackbird', the USAF's record-breaking spy-plane. *Lockheed Aircraft*

First published 1984

ISBN 0 7110 1415 9

Published by Ian Allan Ltd, Shepperton, Surrey; and printed by Ian Allan Printing Ltd at their works at Coombelands in Runnymede, England.

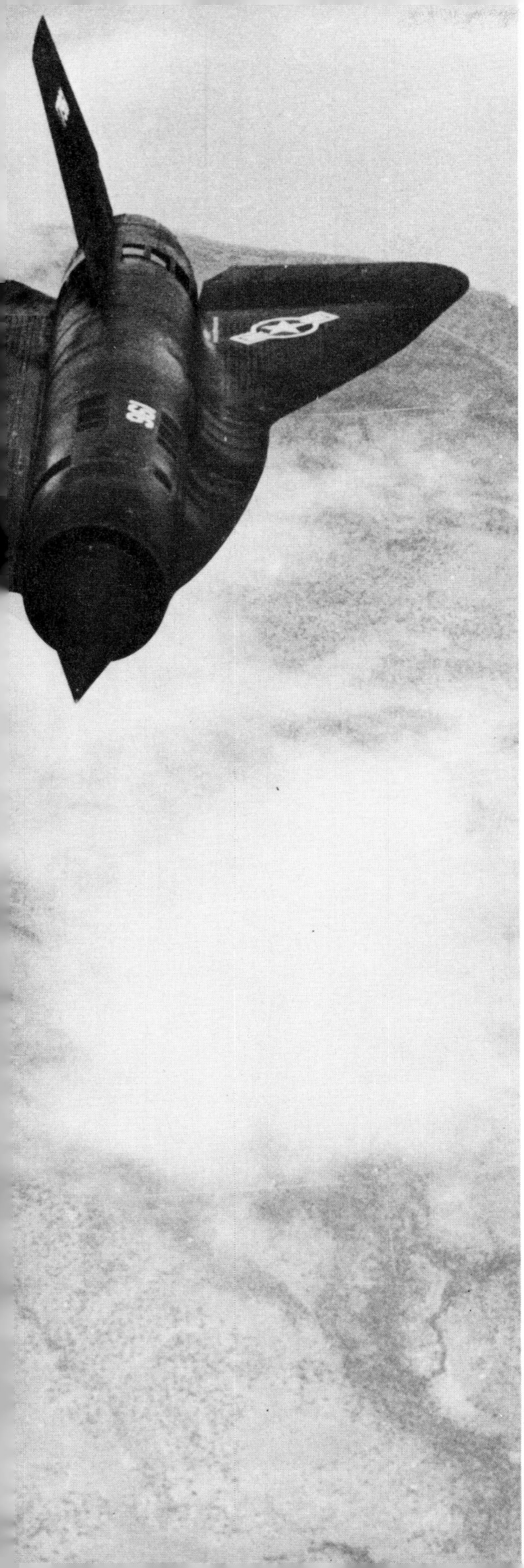

Contents

All photographs by Peter R. March except where otherwise credited.

Bang! You're alive

Bryan Philpott

Above:
The first underwater ejection was made from a Westland Wyvern similar to this aircraft now in the Fleet Air Arm Museum.

On 30 May 1949 Jo Lancaster, a former RAF bomber pilot, was test flying the revolutionary Armstrong Whitworth AW52 flying wing, when asymmetric flutter developed causing the aircraft to become uncontrollable. It soon became obvious to the pilot, who was being buffeted about unmercifully, that the AW52 was beyond help. Reaching above his head he pulled down the face-blind of his ejection seat and stepped into history.

Jo Lancaster became the first man to use a Martin-Baker ejection seat to save his life in a genuine emergency. The escape occurred at 5,000ft at a speed approaching 300mph. Separation from the seat and deployment of the parachute was carried out manually and Jo landed quite safely, albeit suffering from bruises and a slight fracture of a bone in the spine. Three months later he was back in the air following his chosen profession of test pilot, which in the years to come was to bring him other emergencies none of which caused him to require the use of the ejection seat in returning to terra firma.

Some 35 years later over 5,000 airmen have used the Martin-Baker seat to save their lives, the latest models being a far cry from the early seat which Jo used to write a significant chapter in aviation history. Development of the ejection seat can be traced back to prewar days when a young RAF officer considered the problems of escape from a diving biplane fighter when the speed of over 150mph might prevent the pilot from diving over the side. During the war the Germans carried out many experiments using levers and a compressed air operated seat. Over 60 Luftwaffe aircrew are known to have escaped from their stricken aircraft this way.

Postwar Martin-Baker, under the guidance of the late Sir James Martin, developed the ejection seat from the simple unit as used by Jo Lancaster, through a range of increasingly improved units covering seats that could be used at ground level, rocket powered seats, a barostatically controlled automatic release of the occupant and parachute, and even a seat that was safe to use under-water. The short deck of an aircraft carrier did not seem the most inviting landing space for a jet fighter, and in the early days of jet operations many pilots must have given more than a passing thought to whether or not their ejection seats would work under water if they happened to encounter a problem that deposited them and their aircraft over the side of the carrier.

The first man to put this to the test was Royal Navy pilot Lt B. D. Macfarlane of the Fleet Air Arm whose Wyvern lost power during take-off from HMS *Albion*, and plunged off the catapult into the Mediterranean. Macfarlane was trapped in the cockpit and heard the carrier pass over him as the Wyvern sank. As he was unable to extricate himself from the aircraft he decided that there was nothing to lose by operating the ejection seat. At a depth of about 20ft he pulled the face-blind which operated the firing mechanism and 40 seconds later surfaced to be picked up by a helicopter. At this time, the seat had not been designed to operate underwater, thus Macfarlane like Jo Lancaster, was taking a big step into the unknown. Seats have subsequently been designed to function equally well under water as in the air.

Martin-Baker ejection seats have been fitted to aircraft throughout the world, so pilots of practically every air force have had occasion to thank the Company for saving them from a situation in which escape, without an ejection seat, would have been impossible. One of the many airmen to be thankful for the English designed and produced seat, had an experience similar to that of Lt Macfarlane, but this incident occurred aboard an American carrier in 1966. This is the story of one of those 5,000 who took a 'kick in the pants' and survived.

The US Navy carrier *Franklin D. Roosevelt** was 300 miles northeast of Jacksonville, returning from a seven-month deployment in the Mediterranean. The Air Wing was readied to commence flying off at 13.00hrs and the first two A-1 Skyraiders were spotted on the port and starboard carriers. The piston engined aircraft were launched into the clear blue sky as

Below:
The tiny, cramped flight deck of a modern US carrier leaves little margin for mechanical failure or pilot error.
USS America

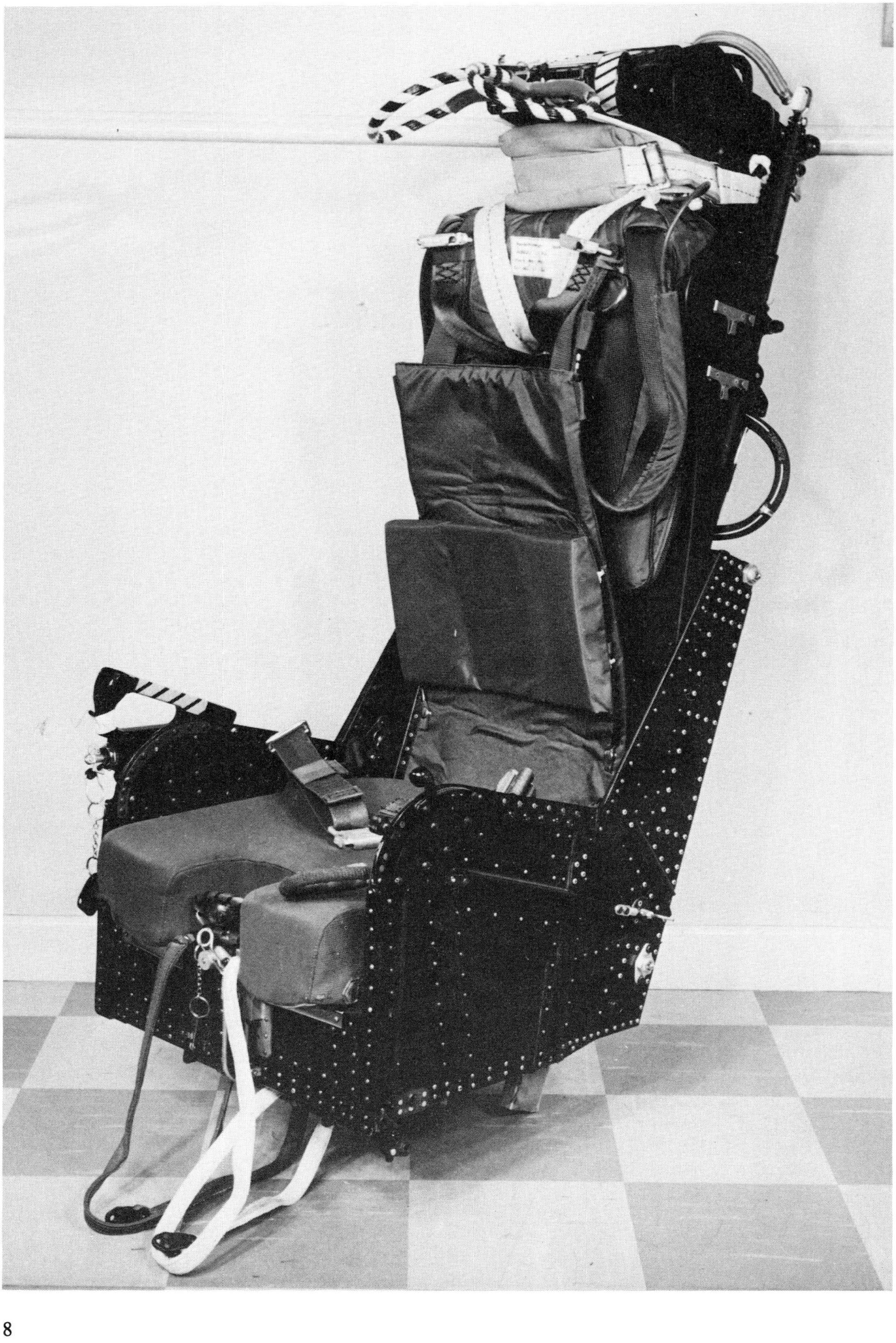

the carrier steaming into wind turned a natural 12kt wind into 32kt across the deck. With the departure of the Skyraiders completed the next group comprising LTV Crusaders moved forward, the squadron CO's aircraft being directed to the port catapult.

The Crusader was fitted with a Martin-Baker Mk 5 ejection seat which had been produced to the requirements of the US Navy and introduced in 1957. It had an 80ft/sec gun, $1\frac{1}{4}$sec time delay with a g switch and barastatic control, duplex drogue system and all the other refinements necessary for use at all speeds and heights. To meet specific American requirements it was strengthened to withstand deceleration loads of 40g instead of the British specification of 25g. Although the initial design, which had been used in the Grumman F 9F-8T Cougar, had been provided with special canopy breaker peaks on the headbox, the majority of later seats had the American system of jettisoning the canopy linked to the firing face-blind.

Cdr Eugene Frazer* completed his cockpit checks, then watched for the signals from the catapult officer; tension on the catapult was checked, and the officer signalled to the pilot to ignite his afterburner. The Crusader's engine belched flame as Fraser complied with his instruction. Satisfied that all was well with his aircraft he tensed himself in his seat, then signalled that he was ready to be launched. The catapult officer pointed forward, leaned over and touched the deck in signal to the catapult crew to launch the fighter. The button was pushed but instead of the Crusader being hurled down the slot in a welter of flame and smoke, it accelerated at a speed that was obvious to the horrified onlookers was not nearly enough to give it sufficient lift to leave the deck. The catapult launch valve had failed to open properly allowing insufficient steam into the mechanism, and the bridle failed to detach.

In the cockpit of the Crusader it became immediately apparent that all was not well with the launch. Cdr Fraser realised that he had suf-

*At the request of the US Naval Safety Centre the names of the carrier and pilot have been changed.

Above:
An F8E Crusader being prepared for a launch aboard the USS *Franklin D. Roosevelt*. *US Navy via R. L. Ward*

Left:
The Martin-Baker Mk 5 seat as fitted to the Crusader. *Martin-Baker*

fered a 'cold-shot'. Within a second he switched off the afterburner, closed the throttle to idle and shut off the engine. By this time the aircraft had moved forward about 22ft, the pilot applied full brakes with no noticeable effect, then tried to slow the Crusader by using the nose wheel steering to pull around towards the centre of the deck, in the hope that he could skid sideways and stop before going over the bow. What he could not know was that the shuttle was still attached to the catapult and the aircraft was being pulled down the deck by steam pressure.

Realising that his attempts to stop were failing, Cdr Fraser decided to eject, but then realised that he would not have enough airspeed or altitude to guarantee a successful ejection. Although having reached up for the face-blind as these thoughts flashed through his mind, he was able to check his actions and decided to take his chance in going over the side with his aircraft. Having made a study of the Crusader, he was of the opinion that there was a good chance of a successful ditching providing the engine was shut down; chances of this with a running engine were very poor. At a glance he saw the RPM was dropping as was the JPT, so these factors also influenced the decision he had taken.

At this time, just prior to the aircraft leaving the carrier, Cdr Fraser made his first mistake, this was in not manually jettisoning his canopy. Although he decided that he should do this, after reaching for the handle, he changed his mind and entered the water with the canopy in place. The subsequent accident investigation panel decided that all his actions to this point had been absolutely correct, but he should have separated the canopy which would have prevented his need to use the ejection seat. Cdr Fraser himself said 'Why I didn't jettison the canopy, I don't known. Perhaps it was fear — wanting to have the capsule closed when I hit the water. I actually believed that my chances of jettisoning the canopy after I hit the water were as good as they would be in the air. And I wanted to know in what attitude I hit the water. I felt that with the canopy off, perhaps I wouldn't know this.'

Eye witnesses estimated that the Crusader was travelling at about 27kt when it left the carrier. It continued over the bow and fell nose down into what had recently been a warm blue inviting ocean, but was now a grey swirling sea. As the water closed over the canopy Cdr Fraser pulled the canopy release, but nothing happened, apart from the front end of the canopy raising slowly then immediately dropping back as water pressure increased.

As the aircraft sank the water became darker and began to enter the cockpit, gradually climb-

The take-off sequence as it should have been:

Bottom left:
Full power from the Crusader . . .

Top left:
. . . the steam catapult propels the aircraft down the deck . . .

Centre left:
The bridle detaches . . .

Below:
. . . and it is airborne.
all US Navy via R. L. Ward

ing the pilot's legs and covering his thighs and the seat pan. Fighting off panic, he again tried to jettison the canopy but realised that the cartridge had fired and was now inoperative, bracing himself against the floor he exerted all his strength in pushing against the plastic cover of his prison, but still could not move it. Taking stock of his situation, Fraser decided that he had either to wait until the pressure inside and out equalised and thought he might assist in this by opening the cockpit vent to allow water in. He then noticed that it seemed to be getting lighter above him and decided that the Crusader was for some reason rising again. At this time he decided that it might be worthwhile using the ejection seat. The aircraft started to sink once again and as water reached up to his chin, he activated the seat by pulling the firing handle. Just prior to taking this action he had considered the possibility of structural damage preventing operation of the seat, the impact rupturing a tank and causing a fire on the surface into which he might be fired, or whether the cockpit area was still sound. But in the split second these thoughts flashed through his mind, the rate of sink increased and the decision to eject was taken.

When the canopy had initially parted from the aircraft, then clamped shut again, it had armed the seat which when activated blasted the canopy free. This was perhaps where lady luck smiled on the Commander, for he failed to operate the canopy interrupter which was the correct procedure when ejecting through a closed canopy. As the seat fired, all thoughts of the closed canopy passed from his mind as he was pushed upwards through the swilling water. He felt himself tumbling in the water and estimated that he completed $2\frac{1}{2}$ turns before popping out and rising some 20ft above the surface.

Once again let the pilot take-up the story, 'I rolled forward, hit back into the water face to, head first, still in the seat. The seat had not separated. Almost immediately on contact with the water, I felt a little charge go off as the seat separated. I went under water a considerable distance. The jolt coming back into it after the ejection was considerable, knocking all the breath out of me. But as I struggled for breath again, I noticed that I was breathing very comfortably under water on my bailout oxygen supply. Although I did not have my helmet visor

down as I probably should have, the water on my face was no problem. But when I hit the water coming back, the curtain still up there on my face, it was one hell of a jolt and it did knock the breath out of me and caused some soreness.'

The curtain he mentions is the face blind of the seat and the emergency oxygen supply was automatically activated as the seat was fired. After the successful separation Cdr Fraser inflated his life-jacket and settled in the water awaiting rescue. He noticed that the carrier was off to his left and moving away. What had happened was that immediately the Crusader had gone over the bow the captain had put the rudder hard over to starboard then to port, thus making the bow miss the aircraft as it settled into the water and making the stern screws turn

away from where the pilot was expected to surface. Cdr Fraser watched the carrier pass some 12 to 14ft away, heard the screws but realised by the position of the carrier that he would miss them, in his words, 'I felt fine!' The next problem was getting rid of his parachute pack which was proving troublesome. The clips failed to respond to his actions and whirlpools created by the passing carrier were beginning to pull him under. One set of clips opened easily but the other refused. He ducked under the water in an attempt to use 'weightlessness' to help, this worked and the pack fell away from him. Now relieved of all the paraphernalia that was necessary for survival in an airborne ejection, he began to relax in the knowledge that there was very little left to add to his problems.

Above:
F8U Crusader over Guantanamo Bay, Cuba.
US Navy via R. L. Ward

By now the carrier was 100yd away, but the downed pilot saw a Seasprite helicopter approaching over its stern and making for him. Despite suffering the final indignity of being pelted by sea water created by the rotor downwash, which penetrated the gap in his helmet where the visor should have been, Cdr Fraser was soon on board and deposited back on the carrier's deck, waving to the pilots of his squadron who had watched in horror as he had disappeared over the side, just four minutes before.

The first VariEze to be seen in the UK was this Swiss example which attracted a great deal of interest at the PFA Rally at Leicester in July 1979. The nosewheel has not collapsed, it has to be retracted when the pilot gets out to avoid the aircraft tipping on its tail. *Andrew March*

Slick shapes

Homebuilt aircraft have made enormous strides since the Flying Fleas of 50 years ago, the postwar Luton Minors and the more recent Evans, Wittman and Bede designs. The revolution in design, materials and assembly of aircraft for amateur constructors has been led by Californian Burt Rutan. From his first design in 1968, the VariViggen, each Rutan aircraft has featured a canard wing, composite materials construction, high performance and excellent fuel economy. Success came with the VariEze (pronounced very-easy) which he designed in 1974, was constructed in 10 weeks and first flown in March 1975. Between 1976 and 1979 Rutan sold over 3,500 plans for the two-seat VariEze to homebuilders all over the world.

This appropriately registered VariEze G-LASS was constructed by Don Foreman and colleagues at Edenbridge and was displayed for the first time in the UK in 1980. Powered by a Continental O-200-A it has a top speed of over 200mph and a range in excess of 1,000 miles. *Andrew March*

Above:
The glass fibre exterior coating gives the VariEze a mirror-like finish which reduces drag considerably. The NASA influenced winglets below the vertical stabilisers show the refinement of Rutan's design technology.

Left:
The Long-EZ followed in 1979 and was an overnight success. It was a larger, more powerful aircraft, incorporating some of the improvements that Rutan had developed from its predecessor. The first UK example, G-RAFT, was again built by Don Foreman.

Bottom left:
One drawback with both the VariEze and the Long-EZ is the small diameter wheels, which makes operations from grass fields almost impossible. The design's fine aerodynamics also results in quite a long take-off run.

The Quickie, claimed to be the highest performing aircraft for its horsepower, also originated with Burt Rutan. He was contracted to provide the initial design which was then developed by the late Tom Jewett and Gene Sheehan. The tiny single-seater was first flown in 1977 and featured a 'biplane canard' configuration with the main wheels housed in the canard wing-tips. It was quickly followed by the two-seat Q-2 designed by the Quickie Aircraft Corporation and first flown on 1 July 1980, taking only four months to build.

Below:
The first Quickie Q-2 to appear in the UK was G-OGKN assembled by Quickie Aircraft (Europe) Ltd at Coventry, which was taken by road to the 1983 PFA Rally at Cranfield.

Bottom:
Powered by a Limbach engine, Mike Sullivan's Q-2 was the first to be airborne in the UK on 14 November 1983 at Elstree.

Above:
Take-off for the tail-dragger, canard Q-2, is called 'levitation' as it literally lifts off the ground at a steep angle.

Below:
The sleek lines of the Q-2 give it a very efficient performance, quoted as max cruise 180mph, max range of 1,000 miles and an economic cruise at 150mph using less than three gallons per hour. *Q-2 Displays*

What's that aircraft?

Wal Gandy

My youthful days had always been happily spent watching trains — steam trains — through the classroom window, and dashing off after school to the local vantage point to watch some more. We knew the busy times and the quiet ones and ate around them. Then sadly steam declined, the new diesels held no excitement, no visual stimulation. So I travelled abroad to see, photograph and travel behind steam; firstly to Europe, which meant ferry crossings via Dover or Harwich. But, as the same inevitable decline spread there, further, wider horizons had to be sought. So it was that I found myself at Heathrow aboard flight SR817 to Geneva, bound for Johannesburg Jan Smuts one summer's evening.

At seven o'clock next morning, I had landed at Kinshasa Airport where all the passengers were disembarked from the Swissair DC-10 flight. There was a problem with an hydraulic pump, hence there would be some delay, to be filled by the arrival of breakfast. It was one of those situations which you know instinctively will not occur again; the opportunity had to be siezed or it will be gone for ever.

Out of interest, I made a note, and photographed, some of the aircraft. Obviously, many were titled 'Air Zaïre' some had names, but all had their individual marks on the side. N747QC I recognised as a 'Jumbo' and there were some smaller airliners: 9Q-CBR turned out to be a DC4, 9Q-CLQ an F-27, 9Q-CLD a Caravelle and 9Q-CNJ a Boeing 737. The 'SGA' cargo plane 9Q-CWN was a Canadair CL44. Not that I recognised any of them then. As the holiday progressed touring around South Africa and Southern Rhodesia, now Zimbabwe, I continued to make notes on the aircraft observed. The bug had bitten. Not that these notes yet made much sense. The problem was how could I decypher them?

Above:
All British civil aircraft registrations commence G- followed by four letters, like this Beech 200 Super King Air G-BJBP.

On my return by Coronado 990 to Heathrow I joined the milling throngs on the viewing terraces. Lots of young enthusiasts with binoculars, all eager to help. From time to time, they checked with a book and cheered. It was the first time they had seen that particular aircraft. Their bible was *Civil Aircraft Markings* containing all the current British and Irish registrations, and those overseas airliners which regularly visit our shores. How could I get hold of one? The spotters quickly answered this —

Above:
The D- prefix shows that this Jodel D120 Paris-Nice is registered in Germany.
Andrew March

Left:
After the letters had been allocated as national prefixes (Z for Zimbabwe being the latest), combinations of numbers and letter were used. 4R-ALC on this Boeing 737 shows that it is registered in Sri Lanka.

Bottom left:
CCCP- on this Aeroflot TU-154B is the cyrillic lettering for USSR.

the terrace shop had a good supply. Leafing through this mine of information I soon discovered that the national marks for each country are allocated under agreement by the International Civil Aviation Organisation. All the British aircraft registrations begin with letter G- for Great Britain, the French begin F- the Germans (Deutschland) D-, Italy I-. There are more than 26 aviating countries in the world, of course, so the majority have two letters before the hyphen: EI- for Eire, LX- for Luxembourg, YU- for Yugoslavia are reasonably obviously derived, but more obscure are EC-for Spain, HB- for Switzerland and PH- for Holland. Numbers also play a part; there are some which combine a number with a letter before the hyphen, ranging from A2- of Botswana to 9Y- for Trinidad and Tobago.

A civil aircraft identity normally comprises five characters, including the national marks. Of course, to many conventions there are exceptions, the most notable of which are Japan, the Soviet Union and The United States of America. Japanese airliners carry four numerals after the national marks JA, while the Soviet Union's aircraft have five numbers after CCCP, which are the Cyrillic letter-shapes for Sovetski Soyuz Socialisti Republiski. Isn't it surprising what peripheral knowledge can be gleaned from the aviation hobby?

Registrations of US aircraft start with the letter N, and are not greater than six characters long, the second character usually being a numeral. There are again exceptions to this, 'C' being used for early 'commercial aircraft' and 'X' for 'experimental' machines. If letters are

Left:
Aircraft registered in the USA have the prefix N followed by up to five numerals and usually ending with one or two letters. N790Z is a BAe HS125-700.

Below:
Amongst the earliest out of sequence British registrations were those allocated to Concordes including G-BOAC shown here. *Andrew March*

Above:
Since 1975 British civil aircraft have been permitted to carry personalised registrations. Colt Executive Aviation's Chief Pilot P(e)ter Turner is recognised on this Beech C-90.

used it is more usual to find them at the end of the registration, eg N1A or N999ZZ. The vastness of that country and the number of privately-owned small aircraft necessitates a wide range and flexibility, and also the re-issue of an aircraft mark. This means that the registration worn today on a Boeing 747 'Jumbo' jet, may next month be allocated to a humble Cessna or Piper.

In Britain, anything powered which flies must be registered with the Civil Aviation Authority (CAA), and have allocated to it, and carry, its individual identity. As well as airliners this includes all private and home-built aircraft, helicopters, hot air balloons, and the modern 'micro-light' machines, although it excludes unpowered gliders. The latter are registered with the British Gliding Association, and are allocated an identity by them. Originally, these were BGA numbers, starting at 101, and had progressed sequentially to over the 2,000 mark when, in 1980, this was changed, and all active gliders were allocated a three-letter identity, starting with AAA and following in sequence. To this day, the wearing of the allocated letters has been very slow to 'catch-on'. Usually the most obvious feature of a British glider is its Competition number, if it has one, or its BGA number in tiny print near the tail-plane, if at all. It should be noted that the Competition number is allocated to a pilot, not a particular glider, and thus it is not a certain means of identifying the glider.

Speaking in general terms, because there always seems to be exceptions to disprove any dogmatic statement, the British Civil Aircraft Register in its present form was started in 1928

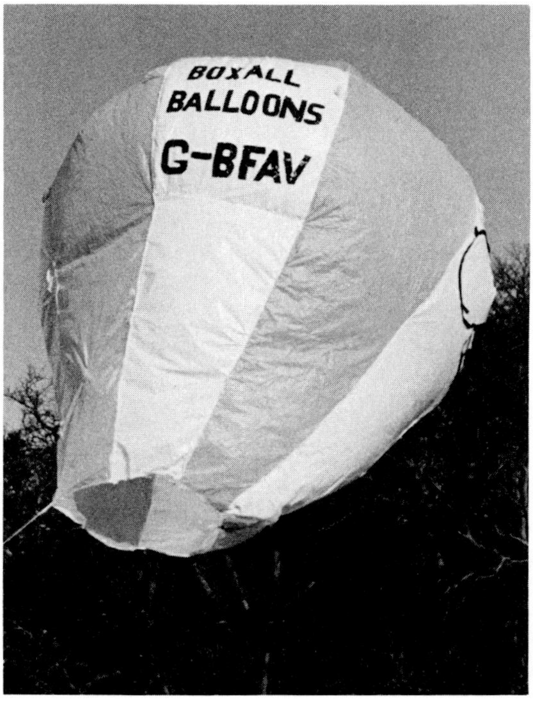

Right:
Even model balloons had to be registered between 1978 and 1982. G-BFAV is an Orion model hot-air balloon.
Andrew March

with G-AAA and proceeded in logical sequence. By 1 January 1975, G-BCVC had been reached, and only 12 registrations 'out-of-sequence' had been issued beyond this; four of them to Concorde aircraft, including G-BSST (British Super-Sonic Transport) carried by the prototype, which is now in the Fleet Air Arm Museum at Yeovilton; G-BOAC for the British Overseas Airways Corporation, which by the time it flew, went to the re-named British Airways anyway, and because of Certification problems for sub-sonic flights within the USA, later became G-N81AC, another anomaly to the British register.

After 1975, and since 1978 particularly, for a fee, anyone could have any registration letters they wished, always provided that they had not previously been issued, or might in some way be considered impolite. This avarice by the CAA and the egotism of the owners and operators, have led to vast numbers of re-registrations, and considerable chaos to the register. It is akin to personalised car number plates. The remarkable decision in 1978, since rescinded, that miniature hot air balloons in excess of 3ft in any one dimension must bear a registration, even though these were incapable of sustained flight or of lifting any weight (sometimes not even

Above:
Mistakes are sometimes made and the same registrations are carried by two aircraft. In 1979 this Piper Chieftain flew with the letters G-RAIN before they were officially allocated . . .

Below:
. . . to this Maule Lunar Rocket.

Above right:
Since 1940 British military aircraft have been allotted serial numbers comprising two letters and three numbers. Hurricane IIc LF363 is flown by the Battle of Britain Memorial Flight.

themselves), brought scores of such craft on to the register, as youngsters sought to get their names via the register into the annual publications.

The final bastion to which the CAA holds firm is the re-issue of previously used registration marks. This is not allowed except where a particular aircraft returns to the UK after registration abroad, is restored after a period of cancellation or the owner wants to re-use a marking that was previously allocated to it. If this rule is ever abandoned, then keeping track of aircraft by British registration identity will become very difficult indeed.

This policy does not apply in some other countries, where for example blocks of registrations may be allocated to an airline, which then applies them to its aircraft. For example, Thai International Airways Boeing 747 aircraft are HS-TGA etc, but these marks used to be worn by their DC-10 fleet. The American register, especially among business jet aircraft, is notorious. The same registration will regularly be issued to an aircraft, then re-issued to another of the same type, then to another of a different type. The only possible way to keep track of these is to learn to identify the precise types by sight, find out the aircraft's construction number from the tie-up lists, published by enthusiasts' groups and regularly monitor the published registration changes.

So far I have not mentioned the other major branch of aviation — military. Surprisingly perhaps, almost as much information is available on the markings carried by service aircraft, at least so far as the 'free' world is concerned. This does not come from official sources but from the publications of amateur enthusiasts' societies and the meticulous detailed observations of their members. There is a *Military Aircraft Markings* book listing current service aircraft likely to be seen in the UK — a sister publication to the long running *Civil Aircraft Markings'*.

In Britain, after a confused beginning, a numbering system for military flying machines was instituted before World War 1. It started with 1 and had reached 10,000 during 1916. A letter prefix was then used, commencing with A1; Z9999 had been reached by 1940 when a double letter prefix was used. From AA100 the sequence has progressed through to the ZE range being currently issued to the latest aircraft. But not every serial is actually allocated because of the policy of having 'blackout blocks'. These gaps were instituted for security reasons so that accurate assessment of numbers or aircraft produced could not easily be obtained by an 'enemy'. There is little need for this today as these details are published by the Government.

Serial numbers are not the only markings carried by UK service aircraft. Many of them are allocated to squadrons which have their own badges and coding systems, so that the markings carried at any one time are unique to that aircraft. The squadron codes can comprise up to three numbers or two letters, and are normally worn on the tail fin or rudder. Aircraft do of course change codes with a squadron, and indeed change squadrons, so although the serial never changes the codes can. Other squadrons

Above:
This captured Argentine Pucara was flown in 1983 by the A&AEE at Boscombe Down in RAF markings with the serial ZD485.

Right:
Hunter T8M XL580 carries the code 719 and tail badge denoting it is operated by the Navy's No 899 Squadron and the fin letters VL show that it is based at RNAS Yeovilton.

have no codes, but apply badges to their aircraft. It is always worthwhile noting a squadron number and code when recording a serial.

The shore-based Royal Navy aircraft often carry a base code in addition to a three-number code such as VL for Yeovilton, CU for Culdrose, PO for Portland. The Sea Harriers and Sea Kings aboard aircraft-carriers have a single-letter code N for *Invincible* and L for *Illustrious*, whilst the Lynx and Wasp helicopters allocated to frigates and destroyers often wear their ship's name below the cockpit door as well as the ship's two-letter code on the tail. The least adorned and seldom seen machines are the camouflaged helicopters of the Army Air Corps squadrons, mostly based in Northern Ireland and with the BAOR in West Germany.

In the training role, the RAF flies the Dominie, Hawk, Jet Provost, Jetstream and Bulldog, the latter on behalf of the Royal Navy and by the various University Air Squadrons. Many of the Volunteer Gliding Schools, giving tuition to Air Training Corps cadets, have the new, powered Venture gliders, whilst others have modern Janus, Valiant and Vanguard gliders which are gradually replacing the long-serving and long-suffering Sedbergh and Cadet gliders.

When an aircraft type has concluded its operational life, some are retained for further non-flying use, and are allocated an 'M' or maintenance number for the RAF, or an 'A' or airframe number if with the Royal Navy. These four-digit numbers are sometimes displayed on the airframes in addition to, or in place of, the true serial. Users are many and varied, from preservation in military museums such as the RAF Museum at Hendon or as camp gate 'guardians', through airfield decoys such as the Lightnings at Wattisham, to engineering training at technical training schools at Halton and Cosford, battle damage repair training, crash rescue training, and fire-fighting practice with fire schools and station fire sections, in which role few survive for long.

Some aircraft may be 'demobilised' and see further flying as private civil aircraft. Of this, the Chipmunk is a good example, and by agreement, these sometimes retain military markings whilst having a current civil identity. In other cases civil aircraft, usual veteran and vintage types, fly in military camouflage schemes of various air forces such as the Luftwaffe, but may only do so with the consent of the air arm concerned and the CAA.

Finally, having dealt with the principal civil and military marks of British-registered aircraft, there only remains the 'B-class' markings. These can be applied alike to either civil or military aircraft and comprise the letter 'G' and a hyphenated number, the first digits denoting the manufacturer and the others the aircraft's identity; for example G-5-10 et seq on the HS125s at Hawarden, the G-27-300 series on the Jaguars for Oman at Warton and the G-31-600s on the Jetstreams at Prestwick. B-class markings are used for the purpose of identifying aircraft that are test-flying prior to the granting of a Certificate of Airworthiness or are destined to go overseas and will not receive UK registration.

Apart from the TTTE (Tri-national Tornado Training Establishment) the Anglo-German-Italian unit at RAF Cottesmore, the only other country having military aircraft regularly based in Britain is the United States, whose Air Force has the exclusive use of several MoD airfields under our NATO commitment. The American Air Force system of allocating identities to its aircraft is quite different from ours. In each fiscal year, serial numbering starts at 0001 and increases in batches as ordered. The full serial is thus the last two digits of the fiscal year followed by the individual number in the batch. For example 82-0650 an A-10A ordered for production in 1982. However, there is no uniformity of the way in which the serials are carried on aircraft and varies by type.

The Phantoms at Alconbury, the A-10s at Woodbridge/Bentwaters, and the F-111s at Upper Heyford and at Lakenheath, all wear on the tail the two-letter base code (AR, WR, UH and LN respectively). Beneath are the last three numbers of the serial, preceded in small size by the letters 'AF' above the last two numbers of the fiscal year. Squadron identity is usually indicated, and most easily identified by fin-tip colours. There is no squadron code letters or

Below:
Retired Canberra TT18 WJ629 is used for training purposes at RAF Chivenor and carries the maintenance number 8747M on its nose.

Bottom:
Piper PA-18 Super Cub G-SCUB is painted up in its former US Army colours as 54-2447. *Andrew March*

Left:
Class B registrations are used by manufacturers for pre-certification flying. This Wessex is using the letters G-17 allocated to Westlands for this purpose.

numbers. The F-5Es based at Alconbury carry the five digits of the serial in comparatively small letters, and no fiscal year information.

C-5 Galaxy, KC-10 Extender, C-130 Hercules, KC-135 Stratotanker and C-141 Starlifter planes regularly visit Mildenhall and Fairford bases. They usually carry a five-figure identity comprising the last figure of the fiscal year and all four digits of the serial. Identities are worn on the tail, and squadron badges for most are carried on the nose. US Army aircraft have five-figure serials, no part of which is relevant to the fiscal year. These aircraft sometimes visit the UK from their West German bases for exercises or take part in air shows. US Navy aeroplanes have six-figure serials, progressively numbered. The aircraft are cluttered with other letters and numbers denoting base code, aircraft type, and squadron identity and code.

The Canadian Air Force which has detachments based in West Germany, uses six-figure serials, the first three numbers of which denote the type of aircraft, for example *104*761 is an F-*104* Starfighter. The West German Air Force uses a simple four number serial system, the first two numbers denoting the aircraft type, for example the F-104 being any between 20 and 26. The Luftwaffe Tornado's based at RAF Cottesmore commence 43 and are among the few aircraft of the air arm to wear codes, for example 4331 which is coded G-36.

The French use a very simple system, taking the manufacturer's construction numbers of built aircraft and part of the serial for an imported aircraft; this sometimes means there are lots of numbers. Therefore type identification is essential. The code system used is often the easiest detail to record, comprising the squadron number followed by the two letters allocated to that aircraft. As with the RAF, these codes are equally liable to change. Our other NATO partners do not adopt uniform systems but do have some semblance of order, again based on aircraft type.

Where to see the aircraft? In this country most of the largest airports such as Heathrow, Gatwick and Manchester have special public viewing facilities, but on a reduced scale today to avoid possible incidents. These international

Below left:
This USAF F-15C Eagle displays the serial 80-005 showing that it was the fifth aircraft purchased in the 1980 fiscal year. The letters BT show that it belongs to the 36th Tactical Fighter Wing at Bitburg AFB, West Germany.

Below:
KC-135A 91484 displays a typical transport/tanker serial number, the first figure showing that it was allocated in the 1959 fiscal year. *Andrew March*

airports are fine for observing civil airliners. The small private planes are dispersed at over 500 locations throughout Britain. Many of the larger ones like Biggin Hill, Prestwick, Coventry and Elstree have regular public parking and viewing areas, and also offer air displays during the summer season.

Military airfields, because of their very function, are less well provided with public facilities. Mildenhall is exceptional and has a small free parking area with boards depicting and detailing the USAF aircraft which can be seen. Some establishments have Open Days during the summer when they open their doors to the public. Then you can wander around some hangars and inspect the aircraft at close quarters. Usually there are examples from overseas air forces in the static aircraft park, and a varied flying display is provided with service and civilian participation. All the services arrange special events — the Royal Navy at Culdrose, Lee-on-Solent, Prestwick, Portland and Yeovilton, the Army at Middle Wallop, the RAF at numerous bases anywhere between St Mawgan and Leuchars, the USAF at Mildenhall, Alconbury, Lakenheath and Upper Heyford. One of the world's biggest air shows has been held every other year at Greenham Common. This International Air Tattoo, organised on behalf of the RAF Benevolent Fund, brings together nearly 400 aircraft from all over the world. In 1985 the event will take place on 13-14 July and will feature tanker aircraft and it is hoped there will be a major participation from the Confederate Air Force from Texas, USA.

The bienniel trade shows at Farnborough, Paris, Hannover and Cranfield afford opportunities to see exactly what is new in the aviation and associated fields. Cranfield, Bedfordshire is also host to the annual home-built aircraft rally when, given good weather, around 700 private aircraft attend during the first weekend in July. Gliding Championships, hot air balloon meets and competitions, and national air races are all well publicised in the specialist journals.

All sorts of information is available from both commercial, and the the many aviation enthusiasts' organisations at home and abroad. There are some books which monitor the British registers of both civil and military aircraft going back as far as the Wright Brothers. Some commercial publications capitalise on nostalgia and review 'extinct' aircraft types. The number of books of photographs is enormous. Some publications specialise by identifying airlines' fleets on a world-wide basis, by listing all the privately owned jet aeroplanes of the world, or by listing each aircraft by its manufacturer's type and construction number. Books of registrations of current aircraft listed alphabetically on a country-by-country basis, or sometimes a group of smaller countries together, are readily available to help you identify and record what you have seen.

If you want to learn more on your next visit to an airport why not talk to the local enthusiast, who is identifiable by binoculars, camera, notebook and an aircraft wave-band radio. Ask the enthusiasts about local flights, excursions, clubs or if you want to range more widely then study the credits in the national publications and write to the editor for names and addresses.

None of us is too old to learn. There is something new just waiting for your initiative to seek it. I hope you have many hours of good spotting. But beware, this hobby is highly infectious!

Below:
West German military aircraft like this F-104 Starfighter have a four-figure serial number running in sequential blocks.

Blackbird:

The SR-71 reviewed

The Lockheed SR-71, unofficially known as the 'Blackbird', was developed from the YF-12A as a long-range, advanced strategic reconnaissance aircraft. It can perform both pre-attack and post-attack strategic reconnaissance missions.

As the first operational airplane capable of flying above Mach 3, the SR-71 pioneered flight at altitudes over 85,000ft (26,000m) with sustained speeds of more than 2,000mph (3,200km/h). It has flown thousands of hours at those speeds since it was introduced to the United States Air Force's Strategic Air Command in 1966.

Left:
Not many can look down on the SR-71 in flight except the tanker boom operator. *Lockheed Aircraft*

Below:
Finals to land.

The aircraft is manufactured from titanium, a major technical breakthrough, and can withstand the very high temperatures of Mach 3 flight. Development of high temperature fuels, sealants, lubricants, wiring and components to operate in this environment was a milestone in the annals of aviation.

SR-71 development began in February 1963, and in January 1966 the first SR-71A was delivered to the 9th Strategic Reconnaissance Wing at Beale Air Force Base, Ca. When President Johnson announced the SR-71's existence on 24 July 1964, he stated: 'The system will be used during periods of military hostilities and in other situations in which US forces may be confronting foreign military forces . . .'

Each of the two J58 turbojet engines is housed in a large nacelle mounted away from the fuselage on either side of the aircraft's delta

17980
U.S. AIR FORCE

17980
U.S. AIR FORCE

wing. Aerial refuelling from Boeing KC-135Q tankers gives the SR-71 global range.

The SR-71 carries a wide variety of advanced observation equipment from battlefield surveillance systems to multiple-sensor, high-performance systems capable of specialised surveillance. It can survey 100,000sq miles of the earth's surface in one hour from an altitude of 80,000ft.

The aircraft carries a crew of two in tandem seats. When preparing for a flight, crew members report to the wing's unique physiological support division for a preflight physical, high protein meal and several briefings on weather and special mission characteristics.

When this is completed, they are helped into their special flight gear by physiological support technicians who will stay with them until they are aboard the SR-71 and connected to its life-support systems.

In September 1974 an SR-71A established two world speed records in less than two weeks. On 1 September the aircraft flew 3,490 miles from New York to London in 1hr 54min

Left:
Fly-by.

Below left:
Overshoot.

Below:
Wheels up.

56.4sec, with an average ground speed of 1,806.987mph. On 13 September the same aircraft flew 5,645 miles from London to Los Angeles in 3hr 47min. The slower average ground speed of 1,480mph was due to an added aerial refuelling. The SR-71 arrived, by local time, almost four hours before its departure from London.

Three SR-71s flown by three different crews set seven new world speed and altitude records on 17 and 28 July 1976. They recaptured three records from the Russian MIG-25 'Foxbat' and bettered four records held by the Lockheed/USAF YF-12A. These included absolute and two class records of 2,092.29mph (3,347.66km/h) over a 1,000km closed circuit course. For speed over a straight course, the SR-71 set absolute and class records of 2,193.16mph (3,509.06km/h). And for altitude in level flight, it set absolute and class records of 85,068.99ft (25,929m).

This sensational black-painted bird operates over Europe from its base at RAF Mildenhall, Suffolk, where it can be seen slipping in and out on its clandestine missions. On rare occasions it puts in appearances at airshows at its home base and other USAF operated fields in the UK. The accompanying photographs were mostly taken on one such visit to RAF Greenham Common for the International Air Tattoo.

Above:
Coming through.

Below:
Gone!

Right:
SR-71 17972 landing at Farnborough in September 1974 after flying from New York to London in 1hr 55min 45sec. *MOD(PE) RAE*

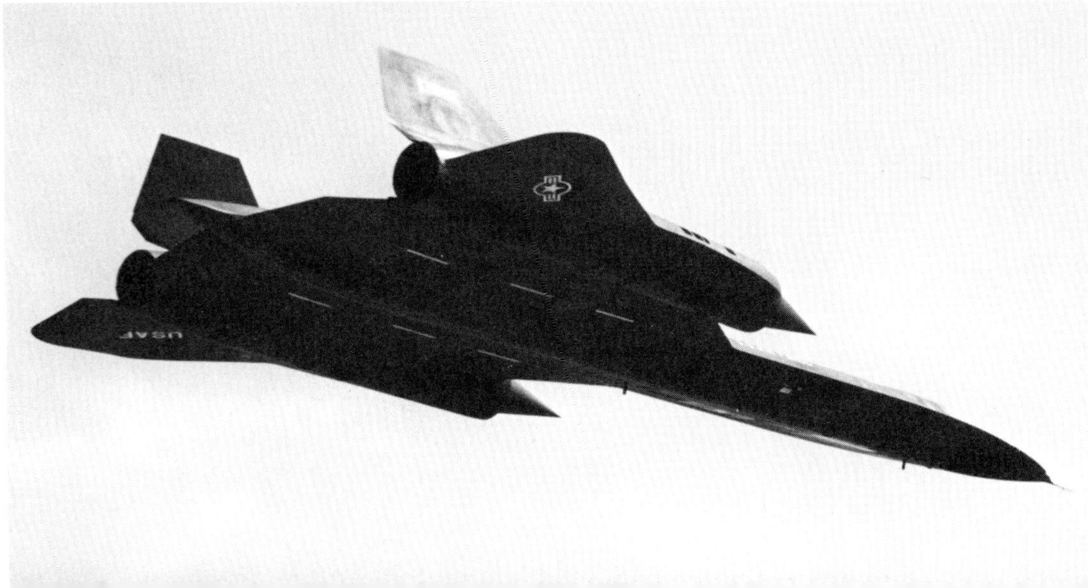

gallery:1

De Havilland days

Seventy-five years ago on 10 September 1910 Geoffrey de Havilland successfully flew his own biplane at Seven Barrows. Sixty-five years ago on 25 September 1920 he founded the de Havilland Aircraft Co Ltd at Stag Lane, Edgware, moving to Hatfield 10 years later. Neither the company nor the original airfield remain but the products of that genius and his colleagues are with us as a fitting memorial today.

Above:
The DH80A Puss Moth dates from 1930 and was flown by a number of the contemporary pioneers including Bert Hinkler, C. J. Melrose, Jim Mollison and Amy Johnson.

Below:
De Havilland's most famous biplane, the DH82A Tiger Moth. Over 8,000 were manufactured between 1934 and 1945, providing the RAF's elementary trainer until 1950 and subsequently the backbone of UK civilian flying clubs.

Above:
The first DH87 Hornet Moth, flown by Geoffrey de Havilland on 9 May 1934, was the last of a successful line of light cabin monoplanes.

Left:
Postwar airliners included the DH114 Heron, the prototype G-ALZL flying for the first time 35 years ago on 10 May 1950. A small number remain in service today.

Bottom left:
The DH115 Vampire T11 also dates back 35 years, flying on 15 November 1950 from Christchurch. It was later to become the RAF's advanced pilot trainer.

Overleaf, top:
DH60G Gipsy Moth G-ATBL was originally delivered to Switzerland in 1934 as HB-OBA but returned to England in 1965 where it was restored by Cliff Lovell. It now lives with the de Havilland Collection at Old Warden.

Overleaf, bottom:
The most famous of de Havilland's biplane airliners was undoubtedly the DH89 Dragon Rapide which was first flown from Hatfield on 17 April 1934. G-AKOE, built as a Dominie for the RAF, is the last remaining Gipsy Queen 2-powered Rapide Mk 4 in the UK. *R. A. Nicolls*

G-ATBL

British
airways

gallery: 2

Propliners

The days of the propeller driven airliner are by no means over, as the efficiency of the turboshaft engine comes into its own. Shorts, British Aerospace, Fokker, Dornier, Fairchild and de Havilland Canada all lay testimony to a busy market. Some of the early turboprop airliners are still giving stalwart service.

Top:
Two from Shorts: the 30-seat 330 which was first flown on 22 August 1974 and remains in steady production and . . .

Above right:
. . . the 36-seat 360, first flown on 1 June 1981, which is essentially a stretched 330 with a redesigned tail unit.

Right:
Over 300 Fairchild Metros have been built. This Crossair Metro III seats 19 passengers, with a crew of two.

Right:
The Lockheed Electra dates from 1957. Of the 60 that remain in service today, most have been converted for cargo use with large loading doors in the fuselage.

Below:
An outsize descendant from the Bristol Britannia, this Canadair CL44J has a stretched fuselage to accommodate 214 passengers but is now used as a freighter. *Andrew March*

Bottom:
Although the first Fokker F27 Friendship was flown on 24 November 1955 it remains in production 30 years later. G-BMAP is a Series 200 operated by British Midland since 1982.

Overleaf, top:
The 56-seat de Havilland Canada Dash 7 celebrates its 10th anniversary this year. OE-HLS is shown at Innsbruck in the attractive colours of Tyrolean Airways. *Ronald Heron*

Overleaf, bottom:
The world's first turboprop airliner, the Vickers Viscount remains in service today with some two-dozen airlines including British Midland and British Air Ferries in the UK.
Martin Horseman

tyrolean
OE-HLS
tyrolean

BRITISH MIDLAND
BMA

gallery:3
Raspberry ripple

As front-line service aircraft have become more and more drab so the 'test' aircraft operated by the Ministry of Defence (Procurement Executive) have become more colourful. The majority of these machines are painted in a distinctive red, white and blue 'raspberry ripple' scheme.

Above:
Hunter T7 XL564 of the ETPS is one of the last remaining with the MoD(PE) fleet.

Below left:
Communications aircraft like this DH Devon XA880 from the Royal Aircraft Establishment at Llanbedr have also been 'rippled'.

Below right:
Westland Sea King 4X ZB506 is used for research and testing new helicopter radar systems by the Royal Aircraft Establishment at Bedford. *Westland Helicopters*

Bottom:
Westland Gazelle HT3 XZ936 is flown by the ETPS to train helicopter test pilots. *MOD(PE) A&AEE*

Top left:
Phantom FG1 XT597 is operated by the Aircraft & Armament Experimental Establishment at Boscombe Down.

Bottom left:
The Empire Test Pilot's School at Boscombe Down flies three Hawk T1s. *MOD(PE) A&AEE*

Right:

Showing just how colourful the paint scheme really is on both large and small aircraft are the ex-BOAC Comet 4 XV814 used as a flying laboratory by the RAE at Farnborough. *MOD(PE) RAE and . . .*

Below:

. . . the ETPS Jaguar T2 XX915, photographed at Farnborough in 1976 when the new colours were introduced for the first time.
Martin Horseman

814

EMPIRE TEST PILOTS SCHOOL

gallery:4

737=1,000

After the runaway success of the Boeing 727 the twin-engined 737 is the second in the family to achieve sales in excess of 1,000. The Boeing 737 order book exceeded 1,000 in December 1983 and has continued to build up since then. The following photographs show 737s of the many airlines that use the type from UK airports.

Top left:
Boeing 737-236 G-BGDR *River Bann* of British Airways landing at Gatwick. *Daniel March*

Centre left:
Monarch's G-DWHH, a 737-2T7, on approach to Gatwick.
Daniel March

Bottom left:
Transavia's 737-2K2 PH-TVP in the markings of Air Malta at Bristol-Lulsgate.

Above right:
Landing at Heathrow is Lufthansa's 737-230 D-ABHL.

Centre right:
Orion Airway's G-BKMS, a Model 2K8, on finals at Bristol-Lulsgate.

Below:
Taxying out for take-off at Gatwick, Dan Air's 737-2L9 G-BICV. *Daniel March*

Overleaf, top:
Air Europe received G-BMHG its first 737-2S3 in 1979, entering service on 4 May. *Boeing*

Overleaf, bottom:
Britannia Airways' 737-204 ADV G-BGYK *R. J. Mitchell* landing at Leeds/Bradford. *Colin Addison*

air europe
air europe
G-BMHC

Britannia

Fighting 56

Peter R. March

Throughout its long history No 56 Fighter Squadron has had a distinguished service record. The squadron was formed under the parentage of No 28 Squadron at Gosport on 8 June 1916, and then moved to London Colney on 14 July 1916 as an independent squadron, where it received its first machine — a BE2C on the 7 August. On 7 April 1917 it moved to France where the unit was stationed at various aerodromes until the Armistice, achieving a tremendous war record flying mostly in SE5s and accounted for a total of 427 enemy aircraft destroyed. Two famous 'Aces' who served with the squadron were McCudden (total of 50 victories), B Flight Commander from 15 August 1917 to 5 March 1918, and Ball (total of 44 victories), A Flight Commander from 26 February 1917 until his death on 7 May 1917. Both these pilots were awarded the VC, DSO and MC.

After the war the squadron was brought home and disbanded on 22 January 1920 only to be re-formed on 1 February 1920 in Egypt, then reduced to a detachment with No 208 Squadron; finally being re-formed at Hawkinge on 1 November 1922 and equipped with Sopwith Snipes.

During the interwar years the squadron flew a variety of aircraft including Gloster Grebes, Bristol Bulldogs, Gloster Gauntlets and Gloster Gladiators. The squadron competed successfully in many flying competitions and also the Hendon Air Displays.

At the outbreak of World War 2 No 56 Squadron was based at North Weald with Hurricanes. One flight moved to France after

Left:
This BE2C was used for training at London Colney before No 56 Squadron equipped with SE5As in March 1917. *Air Ministry*

Above:
A line up of No 56 Squadron's Sopwith Snipes at Aboukir, Egypt in 1921. *Air Ministry*

Right:
The Squadron's Bristol Bulldog IIA's lined up at North Weald in 1935. *RAF Wattisham*

Overleaf, top:
Lightning F3 XR718, one of the Mark which equipped No 56 Squadron between 1965 and 1971.
Richard Wilson

Overleaf, bottom:
High over the North Sea, Phantom FGR2 XV404 on a combat air patrol exercise in January 1983.

the German break-through and destroyed 13 aircraft in one week. The squadron covered the Dunkirk evacuation and then fought in the Battle of Britain. In 1941 it was re-equipped with Typhoons which were used to good effect for the famous raid on Dieppe in August 1942. 1944 saw the squadron covering the Allied invasion and the subsequent break-out in Normandy. It supported the airborne forces at Arnhem and remained in Europe until the end of the war, advancing with the armies through France and Germany. By VE Day the squadron had claimed 130 enemy aircraft destroyed and 63 flying bombs.

After the war No 56 equipped with Meteor F3s at Bentwaters and arrived at Wattisham on 20 December 1946. A very harsh winter and poor runway conditions made this a short visit and they transferred to Duxford on 16 April 1947. The following year it took on the high altitude interceptor role, flying Meteor F4s from Thorney Island.

In December 1950 the squadron re-equipped with Meteor F8s and now stationed at Waterbeach was engaged in normal peace time training taking part very successfully in various competitions for flying, air firing and also displays. The squadron was the first to receive the unfortunate Swift in February 1954 but these were withdrawn in March 1955 and the sqaudron reverted to its old Meteor 8s until May 1955 when the first Hunters were introduced. No 56 Squadron's standard was presented on 27 April 1956 by HRH The Duchess of Kent.

The popular Hunter F6s arrived on the squadron in November 1958 and with these aircraft 56(F) moved to Wattisham in July 1959 after nearly eight years at Waterbeach. The next change occurred on 14 December 1960 when the first Lightning F1A XM172 was delivered. It was flown in by Sqn Ldr Peter Hillwood who had been a member of the squadron during the Battle of Britain. After all the F1As had been delivered the squadron worked up to operational status as an all weather fighter squadron, in which role it was declared operational on 14 July 1961.

XV404
B

On 15 August 1961 No 56 Squadron moved to Coltishall while Wattisham's runway was repaired, and it was from here that the squadron started to present itself to the public. During September it took part in the Battle of Britain flypast over London, provided aircraft for aerobatic displays around the country, and also provided the first detachment of Lightnings from Fighter Command to visit Germany. On 16 October 1961 No 56 returned to Wattisham to concentrate its training effort on interceptions against high flying supersonic targets.

At the end of January 1963 the squadron was informed that it had been selected to carry the Fighter Command Formation Aerobatic commitment, and the squadron was withdrawn from operational flying on 1 March 1963 in order that all effort could be directed towards close formation aerobatic practice. In February the first Lightning was modified to trail display smoke. The team became known as the 'Firebirds', and in June 1963 put on its display at the Paris Air Show. Throughout the summer of 1963 the Firebirds gave aerobatic displays up and down the country. On 15 September 1963 the 'Firebirds' took to the air for the last time and the squadron returned to operational training and its duties as a member of the Quick Reaction Alert interception force.

The early Lightnings were replaced by the F3 in 1965 and two years later the squadron moved to Akrotiri, Cyprus, taking over defence of the Sovereign Base Areas from No 29 Squadron. Re-equipped with Lightning F6s by August

Right:
While equipped with Meteor F8s from December 1950 to February 1954 the Squadron was based at Waterbeach, Cambs.

Above:
This rare photograph shows a line-up of No 56's Swift F2s at Waterbeach in March 1955.
RAF Waterbeach

Left:
The *Firebirds* Lightning F1As break to land at RAF Gaydon after completing a display in 1963.

Above:
Under the baking Cyprus sun an armed Lightning F6 is prepared for flight in August 1973.

Left:
No 56 Squadron provided its own target aircraft, Canberra B2 WH666, while based at Akrotiri, Cyprus.

Below left:
Touchdown, Phantom FGR2 XT901 landing at Wattisham in March 1983.

Overleaf:
Two Lightnings, nearer the camera is No 5 Squadron's F3, XR718/P, beyond is No 11 Squadron's F6, XR752.
Flt Lt T. R. Paxton RAF

1972 the squadron had an important part to play during the Cyprus coup of 1974, some 200 sorties being flown to protect the SBA airspace. No 56 Squadron returned to Wattisham in January 1975 but 18 months later handed over its Standard to a new squadron at Coningsby. On 8 July 1976 the Phantom equipped squadron arrived at Wattisham and became fully operational on 13 September 1976.

The aircraft flown by No 56 Squadron, right through to the Phantoms of the present day, have long been identified by their distinctive unit markings. The red and white checkered band, carried across the top of the F-4's fin on the radar warning receiver, dates back to the 1925. In that year Fighter Command approved the identification of squadrons by painting lines and insignia on aircraft wings and fuselages; No 56 adopted red and white checks. The squadron's phoenix crest, carried on the side of the Phantom's nose, just forward of the cockpit, dates back 60 years. When the squadron emerged in 1923 to be one of the established units in Fighter Command, the CO Sir Charles Bland adopted the rising phoenix as an unofficial symbol. This was authorised in 1928 together with the motto *Quid Si Coelum Ruat* (What though the heavens fall), though it was not until 13 October 1938 that the C-in-C Air Marshal Sir Hugh Dowding presented the squadron with its unit badge. And in the following years No 56 Squadron certainly kept on rising up out of the ashes despite everything that was thrown at it by the Luftwaffe.

P

Bristol's 75 years

A commemorative survey

In February 1910 an aircraft factory was set up in two sheds in the village of Filton in south Gloucestershire, not far from Bristol. This small works, a former tramcar depot, was the seedbed of a tradition. It was the birthplace of a company and a name — 'Bristol' — that are honoured and respected the world over. Today, work still goes on in the two sheds but they are now surrounded by a vast complex of factories, offices, laboratories, testbeds, airfield and other facilities spreading over hundreds of acres of ground on the northern outskirts of Bristol. Here, 75 years later some 20,000 people earn their living with the two companies, British Aerospace and Rolls-Royce, which now embody the 'Bristol' tradition.

Neither the Bristol tradition nor the factories at Filton and Patchway would exist save for the imagination and drive of the man who began it all in 1910, Sir George White. A wealthy Bristol businessman and a practical visionary he had already exploited the possibilities of tramways and motor buses both in Bristol and elsewhere. He was quick to see the potential of the aeroplane, not merely as a sporting vehicle but as a revolutionary form of military and civil transport. Many enthusiastic pioneers of those days 'went into aviation'. Sir George went into the aviation business, and with a world market as his target he named his company the Bristol and Colonial Aeroplane Company Limited.

Within a few months, Bristol Boxkite biplanes were coming off a well-organised production line in the Filton factory at the rate of two a week. At the 1910 autumn manoeuvres on Salisbury Plain, the Boxkite operated successfully, and, in the view of some military men, unsportingly in the aerial reconnaissance role. In

Left:
Looking just like a Farman, the 1910-designed Bristol Boxkite getting airborne.

Above:
This Scout D N5393 was delivered to the RNAS in November 1916.

Below:
Built in 1919 Bristol Fighter J6586 had special equipment for service on the North-West Frontier of India.

All photographs, except where credited, *Bristol Collection*

November of that year the company landed its first export order — eight Boxkites for Russia. To cater for the growing numbers of aspiring pilots the company opened its own training establishments, and many men who later became famous as war aces or leaders in aviation first learned to fly at the Bristol schools at Larkhill and Brooklands.

From 1914 onwards, the development of the company followed a clearly discernible pattern. Periods of explosive expansion in wartime were succeeded by periods of difficult readjustment to the lesser, and less urgent, demands of peacetime. The first Bristol aircraft to be ordered in quantity for service in World War 1 was the Scout, a single-seat biplane with a top speed of about 100mph. It did sterling work as a reconnaissance, training and communications aircraft but it was not designed for offensive operations.

Zeppelin raids and the growing ascendancy

Overleaf, top:
The Shuttleworth Collection's Bristol Boxkite replica BAPC-2, built in 1964, making a nostalgic flight at Filton in June 1968. *Rolls-Royce*

Overleaf, bottom:
Bristol Type 170 Freighter 31 G-AINL, one of 214 built between December 1945 and March 1958. *Roy Bonser*

G-AINL

Left:
The third prototype Braemar bomber was completed as the Pullman 14-seat transport and flown in May 1920.

Below:
Fitted with the Bristol Lucifer engine the one-off M1D G-EAVP was raced in 1922-23.

of the more heavily-armed German aircraft over the Western Front pinpointed the need for a genuine fighter. Filton's answer was the two-seat Bristol Fighter, one of a long line of successful designs by the great F. S. Barnwell and among the most famous military aircraft ever produced. It immediately proved its worth in air battles over France, and its feats in that and other theatres of war carried the name of 'Bristol' to the far corners of the earth. In total, about 5,300 Fighters were built, many of them by motor manufacturers and other companies working under a forerunner of the later 'shadow factory' scheme.

In the final year of the war, the company produced 2,000 aeroplanes from its own factories. At the time of the Armistice, the payroll had risen to 3,000 — compared with 200 in August 1914 — and the original two modest sheds were now part of a factory with eight acres of floor space. There now followed what was in many respects the most difficult decade in the history of the company, renamed in 1920 the Bristol Aeroplane Co. Diversification was one of the expedients adopted to keep the nucleus of a skilled workforce in being at Filton during the economic depression that followed the brief postwar boom. Aircraft manufacture was augmented by production of bus and coach bodies, and later of motor car bodies. Fortunately the Fighter was selected by the RAF in 1919 as the standard army co-operation machine. Construction of new Fighters and the reconditioning of existing ones to meet this requirement brought a steady flow of work to the Filton shops.

The Bristol board's decision in 1920 to acquire the Cosmos Engineering Company was to have far-reaching consequences. Led by Mr

Left:
What a shape! Probably the ugliest Bristol design, the 1922 Type 72 Racing Monoplane only made seven flights and was abandoned the following year.

Below:
The Bristol Brownie G-EBJK took part in the light aircraft trials at Lympne between 1923 and 1926.

(later Sir Roy) Fedden, the small group of Cosmos engineers had designed the Jupiter and Lucifer air-cooled radial aero-engines and these types were developed to become the first of a long and distinguished line of Bristol engines. From the beginning, the products of the aero-engine department enhanced the reputation of 'Bristol' and, as the result of a network of licence agreements in Europe and elsewhere, contributed substantially to the company's profitability.

It was not until the end of the decade that the next name was added to the list of Bristol aircraft 'classics'. This was the Bristol Bulldog which in 1929 won a fiercely-contested competition for adoption as the RAF's new single-seat day-and-night fighter. Manoeuvrability and maintainability were two qualities that endeared the Bulldog to pilots and ground crews alike. Nearly 450 Bulldogs were produced at Filton from 1929 to 1934, and a number of foreign air forces followed the RAF example in choosing the Bulldog.

In the inter-war period Bristol was closely associated with attempts on the world altitude record. The record changed hands nine times in the 10 years 1928-1938, and on six of these occasions the aircraft was powered by Bristol engines. Twice in 1936 and 1937, the special Bristol Type 138 high-altitude monoplane captured the record for Britain.

British aviation's lean postwar years ended at last in 1935 when the Government launched on the rearmament programme. Bristol, like all the other major aviation companies, was encouraged to expand production and gear up for war. This decision had been left very late but one benefit of the delay was that the RAF was

LLOYD INTERNATIONAL
G-ANCE

MONARCH

Right:
Bristol Bulldog G-ABBB was built in 1930 and retained by the company for engine development work. After many years in store it was flown again on 22 June 1961.

Below:
The Bristol 130 Bombay was first flown in June 1935 but did not enter RAF service until 1939.

re-equipped with technically advanced types of aircraft. One of these was the Blenheim light bomber whose place in aviation history is assured for all time. It had its origins in a twin-engined monoplane design, the Bristol Type 142. A prototype 142 had been ordered by the then Lord Rothermere as a private high-speed transport and was named by him the *Britain First.*

In its airworthiness acceptance trials the 142 demonstrated a top speed of 50mph faster than that of any fighter then in service. When the Air Ministry asked to retain the aircraft for evaluation as a bomber, Lord Rothermere generously presented it to the Air Council. Thereafter, the evolution of the 142 into the Blenheim proceeded rapidly. The speed with which re-equipment decisions were being made and implemented at that time may be judged from the fact that within three months of the 142 acceptance trials in June 1935, Filton had received an order for 150 Blenheims. In the six months from June to December, the workforce grew from 4,200 to more than 8,200, and this expansion in manpower was matched by the expansion in productive capacity.

When war was declared in September 1939, the Bristol Aeroplane Company could claim to have at Filton and Patchway the largest single aviation manufacturing unit in the world. The company occupied hundreds of acres of land, with buildings providing more than 2,500,000 sq ft of covered floor space. Even the rate of growth indicated by these figures had been insufficient to meet all the demands imposed by the rapidly accelerated rearmament programme,

Top left:
Bristol Britannia 102 G-ANCE was flown by Lloyd International after service with BOAC.

Bottom left:
Monarch's G-AOVT was flown to Duxford in June 1975 where it is preserved by the Duxford Aviation Society.
David J. Kingston

Above:
V6083, a Blenheim of No 13 OTU, in 1941.

Right:
Over 5,500 Beaufighters were built in the UK up to September 1945.

and to augment the aviation industry's own efforts the Government enlisted the help of the automobile and other engineering industries. Bristol products, both aircraft and engines, were among the first to be chosen for production in the shadow factories and the company played a leading part in the organisation of this complex and highly successful scheme. Two figures give a measure of the massive contribution made by Bristol to the national war effort, either directly or through the shadow scheme; in all, more than 14,000 Bristol aircraft and well over 100,000 Bristol engines were manufactured.

Three aircraft types which together accounted for the great bulk of Bristol's wartime production were the Blenheim, the Beaufighter and the Beaufort. Like the Blenheim, the Beaufighter would be included in any list of classic British military aircraft. Blenheims rendered valiant service as bombers and army co-operation aircraft in every theatre of war in which the RAF fought, and books could be — and have been — filled with their exploits. A Blenheim made the first aerial sortie of the war when, on 3 September 1939, an aircraft of No 139 Squadron made a photographic reconnaissance flight over the German fleet in the Schillig Roads. On the following day, Blenheims and Wellingtons joined in a mast-height bombing of the pocket battleship, von Scheer.

Both the Beaufort and the Beaufighter owed much to the basic Blenheim design, and both were built in large numbers in Australia, mainly for service in the Far East. Until it was superseded as a front-line torpedo bomber by the Beaufighter, the Beaufort inflicted heavy losses on enemy shipping. Designed to meet the need for a well-armed fighter with long-range capability, the Beaufighter will possibly be best remembered for its successes in high operations over Britain in 1941 when it used early versions of airborne radar to detect and stalk enemy bombers. It was one of the most versatile military aircraft ever produced, and, apart from the night-fighter role, it operated with great success as a torpedo bomber, armed with bombs and rockets, on intruder patrols against enemy transport, tanks and other key targets.

In the closing phases of the war, work was going ahead at Filton on a heavily armed derivative of the Beaufighter, to be named the Buckingham, but the war ended before this type had been produced in any substantial numbers. Once again the company found itself having to

Left:
Only this example of the Type 167 Brabazon was flown (4 September 1949).

cope with the problems of peacetime retrenchment and readjustment.

These problems had been foreseen and plans had been laid to meet them. As before, a policy of diversification was adopted, and the company turned over part of its design and production capacity to such varied projects as cars, factory-built houses (using aluminium supplies from the breaking up of wartime aircraft) and plastic products. A helicopter department was set up and this later became a large self-contained division based at Weston-super-Mare, where the Types 171 Sycamore and 192 Belvedere helicopters were manufactured.

An immediate civil aircraft project was to hand in the Type 170, a freighter derived from the Bombay military transport/bomber, an aircraft that had been designed by Bristol before the war and built by Short Brothers and Harland of Belfast. The Type 170, better known as the Bristol Freighter, or in the passenger version, as the Wayfarer, was certainly no beauty but it proved itself a veritable workhorse of the air. More than 200 were built and served in all parts of the world, and a handful are in operation today. Many thousands of people had their first experience of air travel in flying with their cars in the hold of a Freighter on Silver City car ferry services to and from the Continent.

Far more ambitious was the Brabazon, a large trans-Atlantic airliner project designed to meet one of the postwar requirements formulated by the Brabazon Committee. Filton's

Below:
The Bristol Super-Freighter 32 was widely used as a car ferry between 1953 and 1965.

WARNING

XH379

Top left:
Raoul Hafner designed the Bristol Sycamore for the Bristol Helicopter Department formed in 1944. This HR13, XD186, was used to evaluate the air-sea rescue role for the RAF.

Bottom left:
The twin-rotor Type 173 was the forerunner of the Belvedere which was built for the RAF by Westlands.

Above:
The prototype Britannia G-ALBO making its first flight from Filton on 16 August 1952.

submission for an eight-engined 160-ton aeroplane drew extensively upon design studies that had been made in 1942 for a bomber of similar capacity. In 1945 the company was awarded a prototype contract. Although, for economic and technical reasons, the Brabazon was never used in passenger service and only the first prototype flew, the project taught the aviation industry some valuable lessons.

Basic knowledge gained in the design and construction of the first big British airliner was invaluable not only to Bristol but to the entire British aviation industry.

Bristol applied this basic knowledge to good effect in the turboprop Type 175 Britannia, the first turbine-powered airliner to provide a nonstop service over the North Atlantic. BOAC began Britannia services in February 1957 and for nearly 10 years thereafter Britannias continued to operate in front line airline service. One outstanding feature of the Britannia has been its superlative safety record — for example, not a single passenger was killed or injured in the 135million miles covered by BOAC's Britannia fleet. The 'Whispering Giant' as it was affectionately known also served with the RAF and charter operators until late in the 1970s.

The list of Bristol aircraft ends with two pure research types, the 188 and 221. Both furnished valuable information on the structural and aerodynamic problems associated with supersonic flight. The stainless steel 188 highlighted the difficulties of working in the somewhat intractable material and the experience gained undoubtedly helped to influence the choice of aluminium alloy as the main structural material for the Concorde. The 221, a much-modified version of the Fairey Delta 2, was used to investigate the handling and control characteristics of the Concorde-type slender delta wing.

A postwar development of great significance was the company's entry into the guided missile field. After the intensive research, involving rocket-range tests in this country and Australia, the Bloodhound surface air-to-air guided weapons system was adopted by the RAF. It was a major export success, and in its Mark 2 version the Bloodhound is still in operational service.

Bristol's Guided Weapons team had to design and produce much of the advanced electronic test instrumentation required in the course of development of Bloodhound. The highly specialised skills acquired in this work were later exploited in a variety of successful commercial applications.

Even more significant was the company's work in the development of supersonic transports. In the late 1950s the Bristol aircraft

Below:
Type 188 XF923 was the first Bristol turbojet to fly on 14 April 1962.

Bottom:
The Type 221 WG774 was modified from the Fairey FD2 to flight test the Concorde's ogival wing shape.

design team, under the leadership of Dr Archibald E. Russell (now Sir Archibald), were awarded importand Ministry of Supply contracts for design and feasibility studies in this field and Bristol played a principal role in the evolution of British SST proposals. These activities were taken over by British Aircraft Corporation, and Filton became the British design and production centre for the Concorde, the Anglo-French supersonic airliner.

As a result of the aviation industry mergers of the early 'sixties and of later developments, the Bristol Aeroplane Company is now no longer in operation. In the 50 years up to 1960, the Bristol company produced 15,000 aircraft of 85 different designs, and in addition some 8,000 Bristol aircraft were built under licence in other countries. In its 30 years of engine production about 157,000 Bristol aero-engines were manufactured.

Above:
Concorde G-BSST making its maiden flight from Filton on 9 April 1969.

The works now house the Filton factory of the British Aerospace Civil Aircraft Division, and the Bristol Works of the Dynamic Group. Its former aero-engine works are now the Bristol Engine Group of the Aero Division of Rolls-Royce Limited. The helicopter division is part of the Westland Aircraft Group.

Helicopters apart, 'Bristol' and all that it stood for are thus part of the strength, part of the breadth of experience, of British Aerospace and Rolls-Royce, and the pioneering traditions of Bristol live on.

The 'Butcher Bird'

Bryan Philpott

Above:
An FW190A-3 of 7/JG2. The foot step below the number 11 retracted when the aircraft was in flight.
Bundesarchiv

On the evening of 23 June 1942, the comparative calm of RAF Pembrey in Carmarthenshire was disturbed by a sleek radial-engined fighter which crossed the airfield boundary, pulled-up into a series of victory rolls then, much to the astonishment of the onlookers, lowered its undercarriage and landed. The amazement which greeted this arrival was not altogether surprising as the aircraft was a Focke-Wulf FW190A-3 flown by the Gruppenadjutant of 111/JG2, Oberleutnant Armin Faber. Earlier Faber's staffel 7/JG2 had been in combat with Spitfires of the Exeter-based Czech Wing but the FW190 was undamaged. A simple navigation error in mistaking the Bristol Channel for the English Channel had been the reason for its arrival, which resulted in the RAF receiving a perfect example of an aircraft they had long wanted to evaluate.

Some sources have suggested that Faber, who was an Austrian, purposely defected but this is not so. In fact he later convinced the British that he suffered from epilepsy and was repatriated in 1944, whereupon he continued his uninterrupted career and flew as a fighter pilot until the end of the war. The findings of British experts who carried out a minute examination of Faber's aircraft confirmed the reports that had been forthcoming from RAF pilots about this new Luftwaffe fighter they were meeting in combat and which, the previous autumn had regained the aerial initiative from the Spitfire V, which in turn had outclassed the Bf109F.

In the autumn of 1937 the RLM approached Focke-Wulf Flugzeubau, who at that time were not committed to any other major projects and asked them to design a single-seat fighter to supplement the Messerschmitt Bf109, early versions of which were already in Luftwaffe service. Dipl Ing Kurt Tank the technical director of Focke-Wulf put forward two designs, one using the DB601 liquid-cooled in-line engine and the other a BMW139 radial. Although the low-drag in-line engine was generally favoured in German aviation circles, the continuing demand for the DB601 for Messerschmitt production, resulted in the radial-engined design receiving the go-ahead for development. Tank managed to combine the bulky proportions of the radial with a slim fuselage and wings which were fitted with a wide-track undercarriage, the latter being preferred after a study of landing and general handling accidents, being caused by the narrow track gear of the Bf109.

The prototype FW190V1 made its maiden flight on 1 June 1939 with Hans Sander at the controls, and after five successful flights was handed over to the Luftwaffe test centre at Rechlin. The well-balanced controls and brisk acceleration of the aircraft impressed those who flew it, the only black mark being placed against the poor forward vision, which was in fact later to cause problems to service pilots. A minor problem with the prototype was cockpit overheating, this being caused mainly by the omission of the 10-bladed cooling fan which rotated at six times engine speed and was designed primarily to aid cooling of the rear bank of engine cylinders.

This component was soon available and fitted to the second prototype which was also equipped with armament consisting of two 7.9mm MG17 machine guns, one in each wing root, and two 13mm MG131 machine guns in the top cowling forward of the cockpit. Initial flights took place in October 1939 with only the wing-mounted guns in position. Engine overheating presented a problem despite the addition of the cooling fan and subsequent tests indicated that the ducted spinner fitted to both the V1 and V2 had only a marginal effect on cooling. When the former rejoined the test programme in January 1940 it was fitted with a more conventional spinner which was later adopted as standard.

Soon after the first prototype's maiden flight, a decision had been taken to replace the BMW139 with the heavier BMW801, which possessed greater development potential for the future. The installation of this power unit led to the cockpit being moved farther back and detail design changes being carried out to the airframe. The new cockpit position helped as far as the seepage of exhaust gasses and overheating were concerned. These changes were first seen on the FW190V5, the V3 and V4 having been abandoned, which joined the test programme in

Below:
A JG/54 FW190A-4 about to start another combat patrol during the Russian campaign. *Bundesarchiv*

April 1940 shortly after the V2 had been lost in an accident. Initial results with the FW190 had impressed everyone, not least Hermann Göring and an order for 18 pre-production aircraft was placed.

The first two of the pre-production batch were designated V6 and V7, the V7 being the first BMW801-engined aircraft to be fitted with armament. Escalating weight, which had been foreseen by the design team, resulted in a new longer-span wing of increased area being tried on V5. This was subsequently adopted as standard from the eighth production aircraft onwards. The Luftwaffe was anxious to obtain the new fighter and pressure was put on the Focke-Wulf management to get the aircraft into full-scale production with a view to it entering service in the summer of 1941 and to this end an order for 100 FW190A-1s was placed.

A total of 14 of the original FW190A-0 models was eventually assigned V numbers and used in the test programme, which not only included normal factory testing but also an intensive service evaluation in the hands of selected Luftwaffe pilots. The first production FW190-1, which differed little from the late A-0s, rolled off the production line in the spring of 1941 and the first four aircraft were delivered to the Luftwaffe in June, these being followed by a further 26 before the beginning of July.

Overheating of the BMW801C-1 engine still plagued the aircraft and several early examples

suffered from seizure of the lower cylinders. The fitting of a 12-bladed cooling fan and other modifications went part-way to solving this problem. But it was not until the engine and airframe manufacturers, who had constantly blamed each other for the faults, buried their differences and got together in facing the problem, that the difficulties were finally overcome.

Like the armed versions of the A-0, the A-1 was fitted with four 7.9mm MG17 machine guns, two in the wing roots and two in the forward fuselage top decking. This comparatively light armament brought some criticism but steps were already in hand to fit 20mm MG FF cannons in place of the wing mounted MG17s on the A-2.

Below:
Another A-4, probably of 9/JG2 in France. The stylised bird emblem was used as a protective cover behind the exhaust grid. *Bundesarchiv*

The first A-1s and A-2s were issued to JG26 operating from the Abbeville/St Omer complex near the Belgium border, replacing the unit's Bf109F-2s which had been receiving a severe mauling at the hands of the RAF's Spitfire Vs. In September 1941 the 'Butcher Bird', as the FW190 had become known, encountered RAF fighters in the first major conflict between the Spitfire V and the new radial engined fighter. The German pilots immediately found that the speed of their aircraft gave them a tremendous advantage. They were able to break-off combat at will, the magnificent aileron turns and the aircraft's general stability indicated that they would be able to dictate the fight and would soon regain the initiative wrested by the Spitfire Vs. These thoughts were soon confirmed by increasing aerial victories and the general feeling of euphoria that swept through the Luftwaffe continued to greater heights with the arrival of the A-3 model. Powered by a BMW801Dg engine rated at 1,700hp and armed with two MG FF cannons, now moved outboard from the wing roots, two MG151 20mm cannons in the root positions, and the two fuselage mounted MG17 machine guns, the A-3 became one of the most widely used sub-types produced and was exported to Turkey where they saw some postwar service.

During the escape of the *Scharnhorst* and *Gneisenau* from Brest on 11/12 February 1942, in what has become known as the 'Channel Dash', FW190s provided air cover and in the almost continuous combats of 12 February acquitted themselves well. By July 1942 the FW190A-4 had made its debut and was active with JG26 over Dieppe during the ill-fated Canadian assault on the port. This aircraft was different from the A-3 in that it was fitted with a BMW801D-2 engine with MW50 fuel injection which raised its top speed to 416mph. A tropicalised version of this aircraft was also produced and designated A-4/Trop.

In the same way that the Bf109 and Bf110 had been fitted with various factory conversions and field conversion sets, called Umrüst and Rüstsätzen respectively, the FW190's potential

Above:
FW190A-4 of II/JG2 in France during 1944.
Bundesarchiv

was also exploited resulting in several U and R suffix numbers. One of these resulted in the FW190A-3/U1 in which a fuselage bomb-rack to carry either a 550lb, a 1,100lb or four 110lb bombs was fitted, in place of the wing mounted cannons. The U3 had a different bomb-rack and the U4 was an armed reconnaissance version, in which two Rb12 cameras were mounted in the fuselage. The FW190A-4/U1 was fitted with two bomb racks and retained only its wing-mounted cannon. The U3 retained its standard armament but had increased armour protection for the pilot and it could also carry a 66 Imp gallon fuel tank instead of bombs on its fuselage rack. Wing racks for four 110lb bombs, a centrally mounted fuel tank and full fixed armament, brought about the designation FW190A-4/U8 which could also be modified to carry additional bombs replacing either the central fuel tank or wing-mounted cannons. Although few Rüstsätzen (field modifications) were fitted to the A-4, one of particular interest was the R6 which was the installation of 21cm rocket tubes under the wings. These were used with great effect to break-up formations of heavy USAF bombers.

The A-4 gave way on the production lines to the A-5 which was essentially similar but had improved mountings for its BMW801D-2 engine and was designed with the acceptance of various factory modifications in mind. The main variants of the A-5 were:

FW190A-5/U2
A night fighter with anti-glare shields, exhaust flame dampers, two 66 Imp gallon fuel tanks, and armament restricted to the wing mounted MG151 cannons. Only a few examples were used by JG300 in Wilde Sau (freelance) night fighting.

FW190A-5/U3
A ground support aircraft with a maximum capacity of 2,200lb which could also carry drop tanks in lieu of some bombs. Armament was usually confined to the fuselage mounted MG17s but some aircraft retained full fixed armament.

FW190A-5/U4
A reconnaissance version with two Rb 12 cameras, FuG 17 radio equipment and no wing cannons.

FW190A-5/U8
Provision for two 66 Imp gallon wing tanks plus an ETC500 bomb rack and two wing mounted MG151 cannons, made this a long range fighter-bomber.

FW1901A-5/U13
This was another long-range version which could carry two 66 Imp gallon tanks under the wings and had an ETC501 bomb rack under the fuselage. Armament was two wing-mounted MG151 cannons.

FW190A-5/U14
The first of two versions (the other being the U15) designed to carry a torpedo. This aircraft had a lengthened tail wheel oleo and a fin of increased area. The torpedo was carried on a modified ETC501 fuselage rack and armament was restricted to two wing-mounted MG151s.

FW190A-5/U16
A ground support aircraft armed with two MG17, two MG151 and two MK108 plus improved armour and radio.

Escalating weight began to manifest itself with the late marks of the A-5 and this called for a close look at the design of the wing structure which was modified and tried on the A-5/U10. This proved successful and was fitted to the A-6 version which was to follow the A-5 into production in June 1943. This version was designed mainly with the Eastern Front in mind and was more suited to the addition of field conversions to supplement the normal A-6 armament of two fuselage mounted MG17s and four wing mounted MG151 cannons, these being located in the wing roots and outer bays as on the A-5/U9. The following is a summary of the main R and U modifications applied to the A-6:

Below:
Accessibility to the enormous radial engine was very good, as can be seen by the open panels and hatches of this FW190A-5/U8. *Bundesarchiv*

Above:
This FW190A-8 successfully crash-landed after being the loser in a fight with an Allied aircraft. *Hans Obert*

FW190A-6/R1
The outboard MG151s removed and replaced by a tray under each wing containing a pair of MG151 cannons. This gave the R1 a firepower of, two MG17s and no less than six 20mm MG151 cannons. This armament reduced its speed but gave it an extremely lethal firepower.

FW190A-6/R2
Two 30mm MK108 replaced the pair of MG151s in each wing tray. Total armament two MG17s two MG151s and two MK108s.

FW190A-6/R6
Like the A-4/R6, the aircraft was fitted with 21cm rocket tubes. It retained two fuselage mounted MG17 and two wing root MG151s.

FW190A-6/U3
A fighter bomber with both wing and fuselage bomb racks.

Modifications to the electrics, fitting of FuG16Z and FuG25 radio equipment, the addition of a Revi 16B gunsight and replacement of the fuselage MG17s with 13mm MG131s, turned the A-6 into the A-7, 80 of which were produced in late 1943. The A-7/R2 had the outboard mounted MG151s replaced by externally mounted 30mm MK108s and the A-7/R6 was fitted with 21cm rocket tubes in place of the external cannons. The last version of the A sub-type was the FW190A-8 which had basically the same airframe as the A-7 but was fitted with provision for MW50 power boosting. The 25gal methanol tank for this was located behind the pilot and could be replaced by a conventional fuel tank.

As is only to be expected the A-8 was also fitted with a variety of factory and/or field conversions, among these was a quartet of MG151 cannons mounted under the wings, which together with the wing mounted weapons of the same type, plus the 13mm MG131s in the fuselage, made this version, which was designated A-8/R1 a more than useful *Zerstörer* (Heavy Fighter). The R2 was basically the same aircraft but had the underwing cannon replaced by a pair of 30mm MK108s which in turn were replaced by the slower-firing long barrelled 30mm MK108s on the A-8/R3.

Standard machine gun and cannon armament

was retained for the A-8/R7 but this aircraft had increased armour protection for the pilot. The A-8/R8 was another close-in anti-bomber assault fighter with a pair of 30mm MK108s in addition to the standard pair of MG131s and MG151s. One factory modified version of the A-8 was the A-8/U1 which was a dual-controlled tandem-seat trainer, but this never entered Luftwaffe service and only three were constructed. Several A-8 airframes were used for testing a variety of armament and equipment installations and one of the most interesting of these was one with three 30mm MK103 cannons mounted vertically behind the cockpit and activated by a photo-electric cell when the shadow of the intended victim passed over it.

The next suffix to be used was D, or Dora as it was popularly called. This aircraft was developed from the A and also used as a development machine for the Ta152; it made its debut in August 1944. The FW190D-9 had a lengthened fuselage to accommodate the Jumo 213A liquid-cooled engine which was fitted with an annular radiator giving it the appearance of an air-cooled radial. Armament consisted of fuselage-mounted MG131 machine guns over the engine, and MG151 cannons in the wing roots, it could also be fitted with an ETC504 bomb rack beneath the fuselage as well as under-wing racks. First unit to convert to the new fighter was 111/JG54 and one of their tasks was to provide air cover for Me262s of JG7 during the jet fighters' landing and take-off patterns. Early misgivings about the Ds were soon dispelled when pilots found that it had a much better climb rate and was just as manoeuvrable as the BMW powered models.

Above:
A captured FW190G-3 being flown in spurious Luftwaffe markings. It was evaluated by the USAF which applied the oversize swastika on the tail.

The D-9 was the major production version and was fitted with methanol-water power boosting which raised the output from the engine from 1,776hp to 2,240hp, the methanol-water mixture was carried in a 25 Imp gallon tank installed behind the cockpit and enabled this type of boost to be used for 40min. Early production models had the original flat-topped canopy but this was later replaced by a 'blown' hood which gave better all round visibility.

From December 1944 until the end of hostilities, the FW190D-9 gave a good account of itself and was produced in relatively large numbers, bearing in mind the problems encountered with production and disruption of communications being caused by the Allied bombing campaign. The biggest problem facing the Luftwaffe was not the loss of aircraft but the replacement of experienced pilots and an acute shortage of fuel. During the famous New Year's day operation of 1945 when German fighters carried out mass attacks on Allied airfields during which they inflicted severe losses, they too suffered indirectly as many of their casualties were experienced fighter pilots who could have exploited the potential of the D-9 far better than those left were able to manage.

By the end of the war D-9s were beginning to reach JG301, which was a special Reich defence unit, but by this time lack of pilots and fuel made the effort insignificant. As an example, in April 1945 JG6 commanded by Major Gerhard Barkhorn, had 150 FW190D-9s on strength but could only mount standing patrols of four aircraft.

The D-10, D-11 and D-12 were variants that reached only limited production, the first differing from the D-9 in having its fuselage guns replaced with a 30mm MK108 firing through the propeller boss, the second being a ground attack version, and the last being the same as the D-10 but with a Jumo 213F engine and heavier armour.

The FW190F and G versions were used as ground attack and fighter-bomber aircraft and were produced in some quantity, seeing a lot of

operational work during the last two years of the war. The G-1 had a strengthened under-carriage and could carry a bomb-load of 3,970lb, its armament being confined to a pair of 20mm MG151 cannons. The G-3 was similar but had an additional pair of MG17 machine guns. The G-1 to G-4 series varied only in equipment and bomb rack installations, whilst the G-7 had its tailwheel oleo lengthened to enable it to carry bulky stores; the G-8 was similar but had water-methanol power boost.

The F version, which in fact followed the G, was virtually the same aircraft but with greatly increased armour protection around the cockpit and engine. Gun armament of the F-1, -2 and -3 was the same as the G-3 and they could carry a varied bomb load, a typical example being, one 550lb beneath the fuselage, and four 110lb in pairs under each wing. The F-8 was produced in greater quantity than any other F model, and could be fitted with a variety of weapons including 24 R4M rockets, 14 anti-tank rockets, clusters of six or eight rocket tubes under each wing as well as a selection of anti-personnel bombs.

The G and F series were fitted with a BMW801D engine and appeared to be identical

Below:
Survivor 1 — The only two-seat FW190F-8/U1 is preserved in the St Athan Historic Aircraft Collection.

Above:
This FW190G-3 was photographed in Rumania in 1943, the nose inside a portable servicing hangar.
Bundesarchiv

Top right:
Survivor 2 — The Imperial War Museum at South Lambeth has an FW190A-8 on display.

Right:
Survivor 3 — Across the Channel the Musee de l'Air at Le Bourget has this Nord NC900, a French built FW190.

to the A series, which makes positive identity from photographs difficult unless, of course, the aircraft is carrying external weapons and/or bomb loads; the F however, did have a bulged 'blown' canopy similar to the D-9.

Final version of the FW190 family was the Ta152 which can trace its ancestry to the FW series. The Ta standing for TANK, the surname of the designer of both aircraft. The Ta 152 was also a long-nosed version which initially varied little from the D-9 apart from the fact that its flap and undercarriage systems were changed from hydraulic to electric power. Several versions of the Ta152 were produced but these came too late to have any impact in a war to which the FW190 had already made a major contribution.

Over 20,000 FW190 variants were produced during the war years and the 'Butcher Bird' as it was known, earned a reputation that was second only to the Bf109.

WORLD WAR WAS
N THIS GALLERY
E BATTLE OF

-13

Preserve a Provost

Flt Lt Mike Crymble

On 26 May 1983 piston-engined Percival Provost T1 WW397 was airborne at RAF Lyneham for the first time since October 1969, when it was the last of the type to be retired from service by the RAF. **Flt Lt Mike Crymble** who master-minded the restoration and now owns and flies the veteran training aircraft, describes how he managed to *preserve a Provost.*

During 1978, a number of schemes were under consideration at RAF Lyneham, aimed at improving the involvement of the several thousand personnel on the large, busy station. One of these schemes was to attempt to restore an elderly aircraft, possibly to flying condition. Towards the end of that year, we heard that a Piston Provost (8060M), which had been used as a training aircraft at RAF Halton, was available for disposal. We submitted a bid for the aircraft, ostensibly as a 'gate guardian', and it was allotted to Lyneham in April 1979. On arrival, a brief examination showed the aircraft to be in good structural condition, and relatively free of defects: many rubber-based components such as tyres, fuel tanks and hoses were in poor condition but we believed it was possible to restore the aircraft.

When Provost WW397 arrived at Lyneham I recognised it as the aircraft I had seen as a 15-year old ATC cadet from Northern Ireland on summer camp at RAF Shawbury in 1969. Leafing through its log books I was soon able to piece together its history from its construction in 1954 through its 15 years of service.

Provost T1 WW 397 was built at Luton and was delivered to the Royal Air Force No 12 MU, Kirkbride on 20 September and only nine days later arrived at No 3 FTS Feltwell where it was to serve in its training role for just over $3\frac{1}{2}$ years until Feltwell was closed. It was then stored for 18 months at No 27 MU Shawbury before arriving on 29 October 1959 at RAF Linton-on-Ouse which was the home of No 1 FTS. Early in 1960 WW397 suffered a flying

Left:
The RAF's last airworthy piston-Provost, WW397, photographed at RAF Little Rissington in October 1967.

Above:
Under restoration at RAF Lyneham in 1980.
Mike Crymble

Below:
By early 1982 the work was well advanced.
Mike Crymble

accident, details of which are not known but the starboard mainplane was changed by a team from No 60 MU Church Fenton. In May 1961 the Provost was flown to Shawbury where it was stored until 17 October 1966. WW397 then served with the Central Flying School at Little Rissington. It visited Shawbury twice during its service with CFS, presumably for maintenance, had a brief spell at RAF Acklington in July 1967 and then made a final flight to No 27 MU at Shawbury on 8 August 1969 where it was stored for a couple of months. WW397 then the RAF's last airworthy piston Provost flew from Shawbury to RAF Halton on 30 October 1969 where it was to stay as 8060M firstly as a marshalling and ground running training aircraft for three years, then, with its engine inhibited, as a ground instructional airframe.

Fortunately RAF Halton kept and maintained the full set of documents for the aircraft. An up-to-date F700 and the 4800 series documents were all transferred to Lyneham. Research at RAF Halton, the RAF Museum Hendon, Alvis Ltd of Coventry and BAC Warton produced a complete set of aircraft and engine publications, an SI/STI List, a full set of modification leaflets, and Pilots and Ground Handling Notes.

Examination of the F700 showed that the engine had a major defect, a failed crankcase

Above:
Roll-out for the gleaming 'as new' WW397 came in September 1982. *Andrew March*

Left:
WW397 was shown off for the first time at the Lyneham Families Day on 25 September 1982 alongside its modern counterpart, a Jet Provost T5. *Andrew March*

Right:
Now the owner, Flt Lt Mike Crymble in the cockpit of WW397.

NOE
WW397
NE

NE

stud, and the canopy jettison mechanism was unserviceable; the aircraft had been given regular anti-deterioration servicing. A survey of the aircraft proved the structure to be sound; fuselage frames and longerons were all in good condition, with no signs of cracking or pulled rivets. The fuselage skin was in very good condition, and only very small areas of superficial surface corrosion were noted. Flying control mountings and surfaces were all sound. Mainplane, tailplane and fin structure was all in good condition. Rubber-based components were generally badly deteriorated, and all required repair or replacement. Internally, a full set of instruments and controls were fitted, and seats, harness and crashframe were all serviceable.

Left:
First flight took place from Lyneham on 26 May 1983.

Below:
With its 'Permit to Fly' issued on 1 July, the Provost made its first appearance at an air display at the Badminton Air Day on 17 July.

One of the biggest problems that faced us was the powerplant. The original engine had a major unserviceability and only 37 hours of life remaining. Despite a widespread search, we were unable to locate another engine of the correct Mark number which could be made available. Our research did however, reveal that a number of ex-Sea Prince engines were held at No 16 MU Stafford, awaiting disposal. Among these engines was one (Ser No 577) which was erroneously built to Twin Pioneer (Mk 12507) standard. This engine was returned by the Royal Navy to Stafford and put up for disposal with the Sea Prince engines; it had zero hours use. After a good deal of negotiation we were able to obtain this powerplant, together with a number of items of ground support equipment which greatly assisted our work on the engine and propeller.

We could then set to work knowing that all the essential ingredients were available. A small

Above and right:
Angles on the Provost. *Andrew March*

group of the enthusiastic engineer NCOs and officers, all working in our own time, devoted some 3,500 man hours over the next three years to bring 397 up to flying condition. We were lucky to obtain support from colleagues at other RAF stations, where specialist facilities were needed for testing equipment such as fuel tanks, pneumatic components and instruments. But without the generous support from industry the project could never have been completed.

The aircraft's main and tailplane tyres were unusable. Goodyear and Dunlop were approached for information or possible alternatives but, in the event, Goodyear provided four new mainwheel tyres and Dunlop two tailwheel tyres, free of charge. No 32 MU, St Athan, declared both fuel tanks to be scrap. When approached for advice, the manufacturers, Fireproof Tanks Ltd, offered to recover the tanks, the work being performed as a training job by apprentices. The tanks were

proof-tested by the firm on completion. Again, the work was undertaken free of charge. We were unable to find a took kit with which to remove the propeller; eventually a kit was located, owned by Alvair Ltd of Bagington, Coventry, who kindly lent it to us. Examination and re-certification of the propeller was generously undertaken by Dowty-Rotol, as we had no service facility available to us. The external finish chosen was the original silver with yellow training bands as WW397 was painted, coded N-E, in the mid-50s with No 3 FTS at Feltwell. It was rolled out for public inspection for the first time at Lyneham Families Day on 25 September 1982.

When the Provost reached the stage where a first flight could be anticipated, application was made to fly her as an RAF aeroplane. After a lengthy period of waiting, permission to fly was denied as a matter of MoD policy. We were speechless, and soon realised that she would end up as scrap unless something was done and quickly. So rather than see such a splendid aircraft sent to a premature 'grave', I asked for permission to buy 397 from the Ministry of Defence. This was the only way I could be sure of the plane's fate after all that effort had been put into the restoration.

Above and below:
Provost over Wiltshire — WW397 making an autumn sortie from Lyneham.

Allocated the civil registration G-BKHP on 26 August 1982, we now had to satisfy the paperwork requirements of the Civil Aviation Authority before the Provost could be flown. This was duly completed by 25 May 1983 and on the following day I was airborne for the first time — the culmination of four years' hard work. Other than the inevitable adjustments needed to the controls no problems were encountered and by the end of June I had finished the required test flying programme. Permit to fly PR-933-1 was issued by the CAA on 1 July and WW397 was all set to make its debut at an air show. This came about on 17 July when I flew the Provost into the picturesque Cotswold airstrip for the Badminton Air Day. The interest shown in the Provost by the assembled pilots, enthusiasts and the general public confirmed my long held view that all the effort and sacrifice of time and energy put in by the group of us at Lyneham was fully justified in our quest to 'Preserve a Provost'.

No 9

Patrick Abbott

During the early years of this century many strategists in Britain became worried about the potential threat posed by Germany's rapidly growing fleet of giant airships. Unaware that the unavoidable inflammability of these hydrogen filled giants would in the event prevent them from ever becoming effective bombers, it was believed that their range and weight carrying abilities would make them devastating weapons in the expected conflict. Eventually a belated effort to match the 'Zeppelin menace' was made and Britain's first rigid airship was built. Appropriately named No 1, she was also known — equally appropriately — as the 'Mayfly', since she never took to the air in free flight and was so badly damaged when being brought from her hangar in September 1911 that she could only be scrapped.

There was only a brief period of inactivity, however, before public concern and governmental anxieties forced another attempt to build a British rigid airship. In 1912 a new dirigible was decided upon, to be built by Vickers and designed by H. B. Pratt, assisted by the young Barnes Wallis. The plans were based partly on the experience gained with No 1, but soon also on drawings of the German Army airship Z4, which had landed accidentally at Luneville in April 1913 and been detained by the French authorities long enough for detailed information to be obtained.

Above:
The German Zeppelins frightened the British Government out of its apathy towards the rigid airship.

Above:
No 9 on the ground being prepared for flight.
Imperial War Museum

In June 1913 Vickers received an order from the Admiralty to proceed with the construction of the new airship, which was to be known as 'His Majesty's Airship No 9'. This order became a contract in March of the following year. The order stipulated that the airship should attain a speed of at least 45mph, that she should be capable of lifting a minimum load of 5 tons (subsequently reduced to 3.1 tons), that a one-pounder gun should be mounted in each gondola, as well as two Maxim guns on top of the hull and that she should be able to reach a height of 2,000ft and remain there for at least 30min. Despite the modesty of these requirements work went ahead only slowly and even by the onset of the Great War in August 1914 actual construction had barely begun.

A serious setback occurred in early 1915 when Winston Churchill personally cancelled the project, since he considered other matters to be more important. Although his successor at the Admiralty, Arthur Balfour, reversed this decision a few months later, the sorry story of governmental indecision and industrial inadequacy had taken its inevitable toll. The work of actual assembly did not begin until February 1916 in Barrow and not until November, nearly three and a half years after the original order to commence construction had been given, was she completed. In Germany, by contrast, the Zeppelin Company was at this time producing a new airship every fortnight, each one superior to its predecessors. Their latest airships, those of the L30 class, were larger, faster and far more efficient than the comparatively primitive Z4 on which the new British airship was largely based. This superiority was made obvious about two months before the completion of No 9 when L33, latest of the new 'Super-Zeppelins', landed almost intact in Essex. So impressed with her design was the Admiralty that two almost exact copies were eventually made for British use. R33 and R34 did not appear until after the end of hostilities but they proved to be the most successful airships ever built in Britain, with the possible exception of the much later R100. All this was unforeseen of course in the autumn of 1916, as the first trial flights of No 9 were eagerly awaited.

No 9 was 526ft long and consisted basically of a rigid framework of duralumin girders, covered by a fabric outer cover and containing 17 separate gasbags. From end to end ran a long, narrow keel corridor containing tanks for fuel and water ballast, as well as many smaller items of equipment. Beneath the keel were suspended two cars or gondolas, each containing a control room and two Wolseley Maybach engines driving swivelling propellers mounted on outriggers. Unfortunately, in response to the Admiralty requirements, the whole structure was considerably stronger, and therefore heavier, than was really necessary. Consequently when the airship was finally ready for her official lift and trim tests, on 16 November 1916, the results proved to be extremely disappointing. Far from lifting even the meagre load of 3.1 tons which had been specified in the revised contract, the airship was found to be at least a ton heavier than expected, allowing only about two tons of disposable lift for fuel, ballast, armament, crew and sundries. By comparison, the latest German airships were known to be capable of lifting 10 times this amount.

After hurried consultations between officials and designers, it was agreed that drastic modifications to the airship must be undertaken, to make her lighter. Before this was attempted, however, it was decided that a trial flight in the original condition should be made, in order to discover how the airship handled and what other alterations might be required. A few days later, on 27 November, the weather was deemed favourable and at 9.30am No 9 was taken from her hangar and prepared for flight, despite some minor damage to the forward gondola. Fuel for a possible three hour flight was taken aboard, but distributed with the greater amount forward, to compensate for a tail heavy tendency. A crew of 16, commanded by Capt A. E. D. Masterman and including the chief designer, H. B. Pratt, then took their places as the airship's buoyancy was adjusted. Just after 10.00am she left the ground cleanly and headed towards the open sea but within a few minutes it became clear that something was wrong with the steering. A check soon disclosed that control wires from the after gondola had become loose, so allowing the auxiliary rudders to swing freely. With some difficulty, these were secured and the flight continued slowly over Walney Island and Morecambe Bay at a height of about 900ft. No attempt was made to check the top speed and she was kept to around 35mph, but the engines performed well and tests of the elevators showed an adequate response. Not so satisfactory, however, were the main rudders, coping unaided with directional control, and after only half an

Above:
G. H. Scott, commander of No 9 for its first operational flight.

hour the airship was turned sluggishly around and headed for Barrow, arriving over the airfield at 11.00am. As she reduced speed, excessive lightness caused her to rise abruptly and miss the landing party, so Capt Masterman was obliged to bring her round in a slow circle for a second attempt. This time the trail rope was dropped from the keel, gas was valved and the forward propellers swivelled to force the ship downwards. She descended safely into the care of the waiting landing party and touched ground at 11.30am, having been in the air for not quite an hour and a half.

There followed intensive discussions between all the parties concerned, but as the Vickers management insisted that work on the projected alterations could not begin for some weeks, a compromise was negotiated. The Admiralty agreed to take over the airship officially from 12 December, on the understanding that various modifications would be carried out as soon as possible thereafter, that the specified speed would be reached, and that the guaranteed lift would be obtained by radical alterations, principally of the engine arrangment. Until these conditions could be implemented it was agreed that No 9 should continue in use for test and evaluation.

On the day following this provisional acceptance, 13 December, speed trials were

H.M. RIGID AIRSHIP No 9.

ELEVATION, PLAN, BOW AND STERN VIEWS OF SHIP.

Elevation

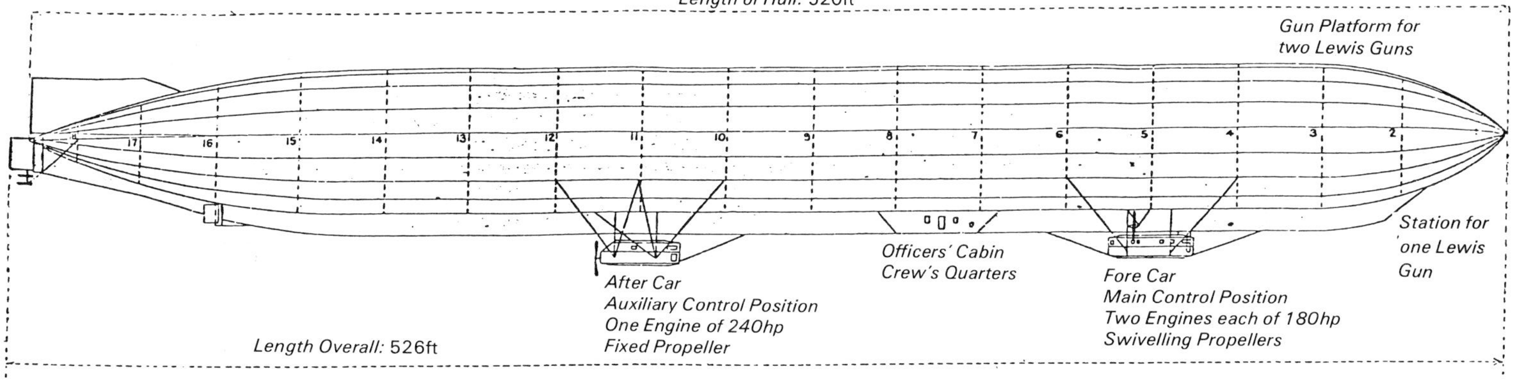

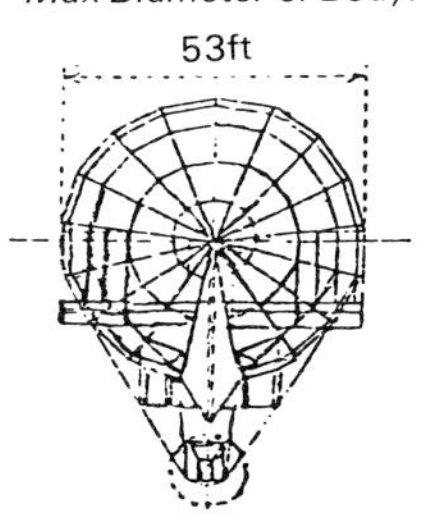

Stern View

Particulars

Length Overall: 526ft

Extreme Width: 53ft

Extreme Height: 76ft 6in

Total Lift at 95% Full: 845,540cu ft/25.6 tons

Armament: Three Lewis Guns

Total Horsepower: 600

Estimated Speed: 45mph

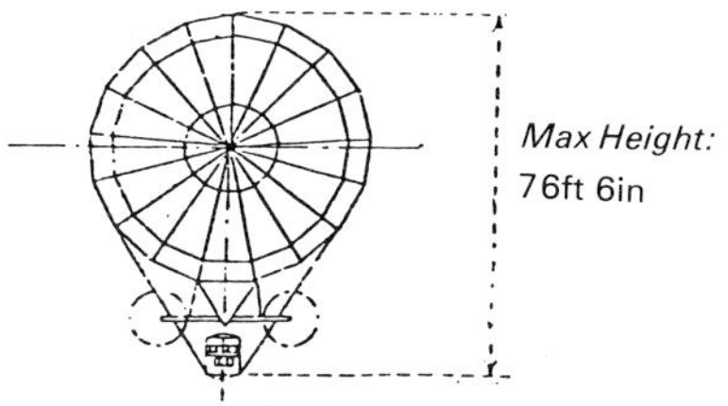

Bow View

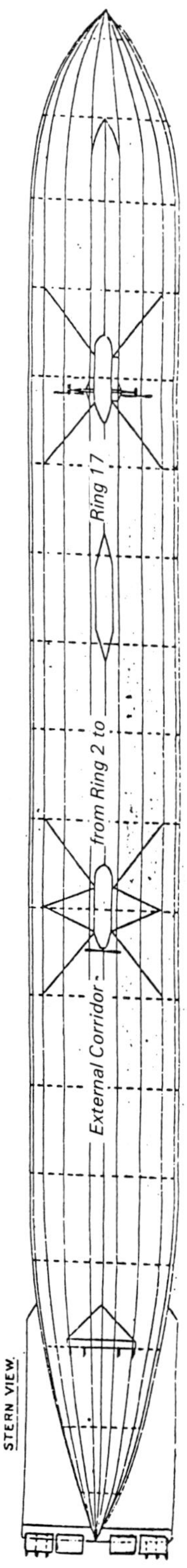

View from Underneath

undertaken. Once again a crew of 16 was aboard but this time Barnes Wallis represented Vickers. The ship lifted off at 10.45am, rose to an altitude of 600ft and first headed northwards before swinging round to fly southwards at full speed over Walney Island along a measured course. Hardly had the northernmost point been passed, however, when the auxiliary rudders again broke loose, exactly as before. Once again, these were secured, but the speed trial was abandoned and No 9 was flown back to the airfield. She was taken into her shed where, following a brief conference, Barnes Wallis won the argument and spent his dinner hour supervising the complete removal of the auxiliary rudders. In the afternoon after replenishing ballast, fuel and gas, the same crew took up No 9 again and headed for the measured course. An improvement in the steering was immediately apparent and the ship duly completed two full speed runs without further incident. After optimistic allowance had been made for irregularities in the course caused by wind variation, the speed was calculated at 42.5mph still somewhat below the specified figure.

On 5 January 1917, No 9 was laid up for various modifications to be carried out, of which the most drastic was the replacement of the two propellers and engines in the after gondola with one fixed propeller driven by a single more powerful Maybach engine which had been salvaged from the stranded Zeppelin L33. Of the other changes, the most effective involved the provision of lighter material for the gasbags: this alteration alone saved 7cwt.

The work took more than two months to carry out and it was not until 17 March that everything was ready for new lift and trim trials. These showed that the modifications, particularly the change of engines, had proved fully justified. The disposable lift was now 3.8 tons, an increase of 1.7 tons and 0.7 tons in excess of the contract. The ship was now rather nose heavy, but this was compensated by fitting another fuel tank aft. All was then ready for the final trial flight which took place on 23 March in fine weather. Cdr W. Hicks commanded the airship on this occasion and 21 passengers and crew were taken aboard. Despite the overall reduction in power, a mean speed of 43mph was attained, showing that the new engine and propeller arrangement was more efficient, as well as

Right:
No 9's forward car or gondola containing the control room. *Imperial War Museum*

lighter, than the old. After this, once a few minor troubles had been rectified, No 9 was considered to be at least fit for active service and on 4 April, nearly four years after being ordered, she left Barrow to fly to Howden in Yorkshire. Piloted once again by Cdr Hicks, she left the ground at 11.20am and made her way eastwards over Carnforth and into Yorkshire. Shortly after passing Leeds, the airship ran into a heavy snow squall, with winds gusting at up to 35mph, which forced her towards the ground at a steep angle. The engines were stopped briefly to allow her to recover the correct trim and after dropping nearly a ton of water ballast, she rose to 2,000ft to escape the storm and made the remainder of her way uneventfully to Howden, arriving there at 2.45pm.

At Howden No 9 became part of Wg Cdr Masterman's Rigid Airship Trial Flight and she was used for experimental work, in addition to training flights and war patrols. No significant changes were made to the airship except to fit her operational armament. Because of the lack of lift this was hopelessly inadequate and consisted of only two Lewis machine guns for defence and three 100lb bombs for attack. By contrast, R33 and R34 soon to be built were each expected to carry several machine guns as well as 20 100lb and four 50lb bombs. It is clear that No 9's vulnerability was sadly matched by complete inability to inflict appreciable damage on an enemy. Nevertheless, at least one operational patrol was carried out when G. H. Scott, who was to attain subsequent fame as the captain of R34, took charge of No 9. Under his command she lifted off on 21 July for an uneventful patrol over the North Sea, arriving back at Howden for a safe night landing after a flight of 26hr 45min during which she covered an estimated 404 miles.

On 6 August No 9 flew to East Fortune, remaining there for a week before returning to Howden. From there, on 29 September, she was put through turning trials which showed that her steering, although improved, was still very erratic. On one occasion she actually commenced a slow speed turn by swinging momentarily in the reverse direction and even when increased speed brought about a tightening the turn, the lack of manoeuvrability was marked. Indeed, to make her swing completely round at nearly full speed required more than five minutes and a turning circle of at least three miles' circumference. Had a hostile submarine ever been encountered, the problems of keeping contact would have been considerable.

Fortunately such a contingency never arose and the only known untoward incident occurred when one of the crew was injured when he lost consciousness and fell from the top of the ship when checking the gasbags for leaks.

On 15 October No 9 flew to Cranwell where she stayed for a week before going back to Howden. She was then used for training and also spent many hours moored out in the open to test various anchoring systems. After the last of these trials she became badly damaged when being taken into her hangar, and Barnes Wallis was asked to carry out repairs and to strengthen the bows. On 20 February 1918 the airship was

transferred to her last station at Pulham, Norfolk, where she was again used for mooring tests, including being tethered to sea anchors in the Wash. In March she also made her last flights, bringing her entire service flying record to 4,508 miles in 198hr 16min. For three more months after this she was laid up in her shed and finally, on 28 June 1918, she was officially deleted and dismantled. Rather ignominously the commanding officer at Pulham retained 20ft of the airship's nose and had the framework erected as a bandstand and rose trellis.

So passed His Majesty's Airship Rigid No 9; a craft built too late and too heavy. She had no sister ship but the later rigid airships built in Britain before the end of the war were mostly improvements on her basic design and performed no great feats. Yet No 9 is still sure of a small niche in aeronautical history; she was the first British rigid airship to fly and the first venture to be associated with the name of Barnes Wallis.

Above:
Looking all of her 526ft length, the No 9 attained a speed of 43mph after modifications. *Science Museum*

Below:
Another view of No 9 being flown by Maj Scott. *Fleet Air Arm Museum*

Military Jetstream

John G. Smith

Designed by Handley Page Ltd as long ago as 1965, the military versions of the Jetstream have since weathered such catastrophies as cancellation of a larger order by the USAF, the aircraft's designers going into liquidation and more than one setback in British military service due to technical problems, defence expenditure curbs, changing requirements and new priorities. It was not until seven years later that the twin turboprop Jetstream was adopted by the RAF and it took a further five years before its military career began to settle down to any extent. This is an account of the rise and fall and subsequent resurrection of the Jetstream in British military service.

The Jetstream was conceived in the early 1960s when, largely due to political decisions, Handley Page's were left very much 'out in the cold' when it came to military contracts. The reasons for this are fairly complex but were in part due to a desire by the Government of the day to see the British aircraft manufacturing industry concentrated into two large groups for airframes and one (Rolls-Royce) for aero-engines. The two large groupings of airframe manufacturers emerged as the British Aircraft Corporation and Hawker Siddeley Aircraft. The Government used the selective issue of military contracts as a stick with which to beat the reluctant aircraft industry into the shape it desired. The head of Handley Page Ltd, Sir Frederick Handley-Page refused to join either of these two groupings on anything other than his own terms. This was partly due to personal animosity between himself and Sir Roy Dobson (Head of Avro and subsequently of Hawker Siddeley) and partly because he considered BAC's offer for his company to be derisory. As retribution for his intransigence Handley Page was given only the very minimum of Government contracts. These mostly related to the maintenance and modification of Victor

Below:
The first military Jetstream T1 was converted from the Cal-State Air Lines N1036S, becoming XX475.
J. Guthrie

Above:
Showing obvious signs of conversion work, XX475 at Prestwick prior to its first flight as a T1. *J. Guthrie*

bombers and tankers. Orders for the Victor B2 were heavily cut back with 25 aircraft being cancelled in August 1960. The 'last straw' came in March 1962, when Handley Page was denied a valuable contract for the Valetta/Dakota replacement requirement. Handley Page had offered a military-freighter version of their HP124 Herald airliner, and this aircraft took part in competitive trials at Martlesham Heath, Suffolk in February 1962. Pitted against the military Herald was a rival design, the Hawker Siddeley (née Avro) HS748MF. In March 1962 the HS748MF was ordered into production as the HS780 Andover C1. Compounding the problem at this time was the disappointing sales record of Handley Page's only civil aircraft programme at that time, the HP124 Dart Herald. This, along with the completion of Victor B2 production, all pointed to the company being seriously short of work in the years ahead. By 1963 it was realised that a new civil aircraft programme would have to be launched urgently if the company's future was to be secured.

After conducting extensive research into the potential markets for civil aircraft and drawing up several design proposals, Handley Page decided to go for the light executive twin market, with the HP137 design being selected for go ahead. At that time, the company had high hopes for the design, later named Jetstream. However it was not to be the resounding success that was the key to survival. Sales were sluggish and disappointing. The best hope for an early large-scale production run, an order for up to 87 aircraft for the USAF as the C-10A, was short-lived. Believed to be offset purchases against the RAF's order for 50 General Dynamics F-111Ks was cancelled when Handley Page's began to run into financial problems in 1968. No doubt the British Government's cancellation of the F-111K in 1968 also had some influence.

These financial problems continued into 1969 and came to a head on 8 August, when an official receiver was called in and Handley Page's were declared bankrupt. There was pressure at that time for the Government to intervene but they only did so to the extent of transferring all Victor back-up programmes to Hawker Siddeley at Woodford. A privately-backed rescue bid was made for the company but this eventually failed and Handley Page Aircraft Ltd, as the company had been renamed, went down for the second and last time on 2 March 1970.

With the final collapse of Handley Page the story of the Jetstream could have, and nearly

did, come to an abrupt end. The Jetstream programme was saved however, through the intervention of Terravia Trading Services Ltd, who rescued 21 Jetstreams and a whole host of spares and incomplete airframes from the receivers at the Radlett works of Handley Page's and removed them to Sywell airfield near Northampton. Terravia then launched a company, Jetstream Aircraft Ltd, to revive and relaunch the Jetstream programme and provide support and back-up for existing Handley-Page built Jetstreams.

The first glimmer of interest by the Ministry of Defence in the Jetstream came when G-AXFV was delivered to the Aeroplane and Armament Experimental Establishment (A&AEE) at Boscombe Down on 9 August 1971. G-AXFV was evaluated in the UK and subsequently under tropical conditions at Dubai and Tehran, Iran, the following month. This interest was part of a preliminary search to find a replacement for the elderly Vickers Varsity in the multi-engined crew trainer role. As part of this preliminary search, the MoD selected four possible candidates for the requirement: the Mitsubishi MU-2, the Swearingen Merlin, the Rockwell Aero Commander 690 and the Jetstream. By the end of 1971 the choice had been reduced still further to just two candidates — the Aero Commander 690 or the Jetstream. In anticipation of further large scale orders, the talk was of 50-60 aircraft for the RAF both civil and military, Terravia Trading Services joined forces with Scottish Aviation Ltd, to form a new company Scottish Jetstream Ltd, on 14 September 1971, with a view to establishing a production line at Scottish Aviation's Prestwick factory, after the 21 salvaged aircraft at Sywell had been refurbished and sold.

Above:
XX478 was delivered to the CFS at Little Rissington on 27 October 1973 for service evaluation.

On 24 February 1972 Mr Ian Gilmour, the then Minister of State for the Defence Procurement Executive, announced that the Jetstream had been selected for the multi-engined navigational trainer role to replace the Vickers Varsity T1 and that 26 aircraft had been ordered on a contract worth some £9million. This contract was formally signed on 22 March 1972. All the aircraft were to be built or rebuilt in the case of the first seven aircraft, at Scottish Aviation's Prestwick works. It was here, on the strength of the order that SAL took over all the design and production rights and set about establishing a Jetstream production line.

The first Jetstream to arrive at Prestwick from Sywell was G-AXUP, the 49th production aircraft which had been in storage at Sywell, which was moved by road to Prestwick in

Above:
The ill-fated XX477, here at Prestwick before delivery to the CFS. *J. Guthrie*

August 1971. It was later to re-emerge as XX481, the 7th Jetstream T1. By May 1972, 18 fuselages and numerous wing sets had arrived at Prestwick, all of them arriving by road except G-AXXS, which was flown from Sywell via Speke to Prestwick on 27 July 1972.

In order to get the Jetstream order for the RAF going as soon as possible whilst the production line was being set up, two aircraft N1036S and N1037S were purchased from the Regency International Corporation in the USA and flown to Prestwick in May 1972 for overhaul and modification to Jetstream T1 standard. They became XX475 and XX476, the first two production Jetstream T1s, there being no 'prototype' as such. Detail changes from the civil Jetstream Series 100 included 'eyebrow' windows, to improve visibility in the banked turn manoeuvre, installation of Astazou XVI-D1 engines and a specialised avionics fitment worth in 1972 terms £252,000. This included a Sperry STARS Flight Director and a Marconi AD370B Aerial Direction Finder, as well as a modified cabin layout with four passenger seats and a toilet.

The first aircraft to be refurbished as a military Jetstream T1 was rolled out for the first time at Prestwick on 26 March 1973, in primer with the RAF serial XX475. After completing compass swings and engine runs XX475 first left the Prestwick runway on 13 April 1973. Following further flight trials by Scottish Aviation and a visit to the paint shop for a spray in the red and white 'trainer' colours, XX475 left Prestwick for the A&AEE at Boscombe Down on 26 July 1973 for general acceptance trials.

By November 1974, 14 of the 26 Jetstream T1s on order had been delivered from Prestwick. This was somewhat behind the original delivery dates specified in the 1972 contract. The slippage had been agreed by the Ministry of Defence as a direct result of the revised and much reduced training requirements, the lingering effects of the three-day working week during the crisis hit days of the winter of 1973-74, and a shortage of certain vital components. The first deliveries of Jetstreams to service units had taken place over a year earlier, when XX476, the second production aircraft, arrived at RAF Little Rissington, Glos on 27 October 1973 for service evaluation by the Central Flying School. Deliveries began to gather pace from then on, mostly to the Central Flying School and to No 5 Flying Training School at RAF Oakington, Cambs. By the autumn of 1974, No 5 FTS had sufficient Jetstreams on its charge to start phasing out its Vickers Varsities and operate its first Jetstream-only training course.

Just as the Jetstream had got itself established in RAF service, defence expenditure cutbacks again began to bite during 1974-75, these giving the Jetstream yet another setback in its already troubled career. When the Jetstream entered RAF service it was planned that many of the pilots being trained on the type would then pro-

Below:
The Multi-engine Training Squadron (METS) was formed at Leeming as part of No 3FTS in 1977, receiving initially seven Jetstream T1s, including XX495.
Roger Lindsay

gress from the No 5 FTS courses to such units as No 46 Squadron (Andover C1s), No 53 Squadron (Belfasts) and Nos 99 and 511 Squadrons (Britannias). As a result of defence expenditure cuts all of these units were disbanded in 1975-76 and the aircraft phased out of service. Hence a large number of already-qualified 'multi-engined' aircrew became available for posting and the RAF found itself over-supplied with pilots and navigators. Consequently it had a very much reduced requirement and therefore decided to end all 'multi-engined' pilot and aircrew training in late 1974 for an indefinite period.

An added blow to the Jetstream was the fact that both of the RAF bases where it was being operated were scheduled to be closed by the end of 1975. As part of the package of defence expenditure cuts No 5 FTS was to be disbanded, and the Central Flying School was to be dispersed. As if all that were not a bad enough setback for the Jetstream's RAF career, the type began to suffer mysterious problems with its engines. An example of this was Jetstream T Mk 1 XX477 '31' of the CFS, which was forced to make an emergency landing at Pershore on 18 October 1974 due to engine failure. Less than three weeks later, on 1 November, the same aircraft suffered an unexpected power loss in both engines whilst performing a practice overshoot at Little Rissington, which caused the aircraft to force-land, causing so much damage, that it was later written off as 'beyond repair'. Later the same day another

Left:
XX481 was the first of the T2s to be delivered to RNAS Culdrose on 26 October 1978, shown here alongside a Sea Prince which it eventually replaced. *RNAS Culdrose*

CFS Jetstream, XX480 '33', suffered a similar sort of power loss on take off, fortunately without sustaining any major damage this time. All Jetstreams were immediately grounded as a result for an indefinite period until the trouble was rooted out.

The winter of 1974 was the beginning of the 'black days' for the RAF's Jetstreams. Without a base, without a unit, and without a purpose, the No 5 FTS Jetstreams were ferried from RAF Oakington to either Little Rissington or No 19 MU, RAF St Athan for storage, pending a decision as to their fate. Throughout 1975, numerous Jetstreams were to be seen out on the airfield at Little Rissington performing engine runs; either to maintain their operational readiness, should they be required to return to service, or to trace the source of the engine power loss problem. At the end of 1975 Little Rissington was itself closed and within a couple of weeks 24 Jetstream T1s had been assembled at RAF St Athan for storage, including several delivered direct from the manufacturers (XX487-XX500). The remaining aircraft XX488 was delivered to Turbomeca at Pau, France in May 1975 for the engine manufacturer to 'have a go' at tracing the engine power loss problem in the Astazou XVI-D1. The fault in the engines was eventually traced to a fuel flow problem which was cured without too much difficulty. Soon afterwards all the Jetstreams in storage at St Athan were modified to eliminate the problem. During 1975, pressure had been applied to the Ministry of Defence by certain Members of Parliament to have some or all of the Jetstreams in storage at St Athan released for refurbishment and resale elsewhere, either on the civil market, or to the Belgian Air Force which was at that time looking for a Jetstream size aircraft to replace the elderly Hunting Pembrokes or to the Iraqi Government, also in the market for a similar aircraft for the light transport/communications role.

Plans to refurbish and resell the Jetstreams elsewhere came to nothing due to the depressed state of the civil aircraft market, the Belgians selecting the Swearingen Merlin, and the Iraqis cancelling their plans for purchase. As a result, the Jetstream remained in the doldrums until January 1976, when XX496 was demonstrated to the Fleet Air Arm at RNAS Culdrose. It was evaluated as a possible replacement for the 1953-54 vintage Hunting Sea Prince T1s in use at that time with No 750 Squadron (The Royal Naval Observer Training School). The demonstration of XX496 was evidently a success, as on 29 October 1976 14 of the stored Jetstreams were ordered to be refurbished for the Royal Navy, designated Jetstream T2. The aircraft selected were XX475-XX476, XX478-XX481, XX483-XX490. The remaining 11 aircraft (XX482 and XX491-XX500) were also reactivated, forming a new Multi Engined Training Squadron (or METS) based at RAF Leeming. The fuselage of the ill-fated Jetstream

Above:
A thimble-nosed T2 of No 750 Squadron flying over RNAS Culdrose in March 1979. *RNAS Culdrose*

Below:
Inside the T2, showing the observer training station (right) and the cockpit (left).

XX477 was also brought out of storage in September 1976, and moved to RAF Finningley for use as a ground simulator (as 8462M).

This new lease of life for the Jetstream's military service built up in late 1976 and into early 1977, so that by April 1977 eight aircraft had been reactivated and direct training courses were being operated at Leeming, both to convert pilots from other types to the multi-engined training syllabus, these pilots being destined to pass on from the METS to the RAF's large aircraft fleet and for direct training of *ab initio* pilots fresh out of the Jet Provost equipped Flying Training Schools. The METS built up to its full strength of 11 aircraft and by 1981 was training 60 new pilots and 45 'refresher' students per year. After the moratorium on pilot training it was re-instated in the late 1970s due to the 'experience gap' opening up in the RAF's strength of qualified multi-engine aircrew. Older, experienced aircrews were either leaving the service or being reposted to non-flying jobs and the more intensive use of the RAF's transport fleet required additional crews to fly them. By early 1979, the RAF's pilot training had been stepped up to such a degree that one of the main training bases, RAF Leeming, was fast approaching its capacity to handle aircraft movements. Consequently, the METS, which was part of No 3 FTS was transferred on 30 April 1979 to the control of No 6 FTS, and moved across to Finningley. Since then, the Jetstreams of the METS have settled down to their necessary, if unglamorous task, and will probably still be in service at the turn of the century.

Most of the aircraft allocated for a career with the Royal Navy were returned to Scottish Aviation at Prestwick between 1977 and 1979 for the fitting of revised avionics, most noticeably a modified radar in a revised 'thimble' nosecone. The first Jetstream T2 to be delivered was XX481, which arrived at RNAS Culdrose on 26 October 1978, piloted by No 750 Squadron's Commanding Officer, Lt Cdr N. L. Featherstone. After that deliveries of the modified aircraft were fairly swift, allowing all of the Sea Princes to be retired from service by April 1979. The Royal Navy later decided that it would need more than the number of aircraft it had first planned for, and consequently, it was decided to increase the fleet from 14 to 16. This was achieved by purchasing two civil Jetstreams (G-AXWO and G-AXFV) for refurbishing as T2s. Serialled ZA110 and ZA111 this final pair was delivered in 1982. Thus equipped with 16 Jetstreams, No 750 Squadron should have sufficient aircraft to facilitate the training requirements of the Royal Naval Observer School for the next 20 years or more.

There has also been one further known proposal for the Jetstream intended for British military service, the Jetstream C3 light transport and communications aircraft. This version of the Jetstream was proposed in response to the Ministry of Defence's Air Staff Target AST408, which was a requirement for a light transport/communications aircraft intended to replace the last of the RAF's distinctly elderly de Havilland Devons and Hunting Pembrokes. Under the terms of AST408 proposals were made early in 1980 to order 18 aircraft and British Aerospace's Scottish Division, the new name for Scottish Aviation after it had been nationalised on 1 April 1977, submitted the latest version of the Jetstream for the AST408 contract. The 1980s version of the Jetstream was the Series 31, an updated version, including such features as Garrett AiResearch TPE-331-10 turboprops in place of the original Turbomeca Astazous, advanced technology propellers, as well as new electrical, air conditioning and cockpit systems. At the time of the first flight of the prototype Jetstream 31, G-JSSD (a conversion from G-AXJZ) on 28 March 1980, the terms of reference of AST408 required that the aircraft selected should be in service by January 1982 — which was some months in advance of the scheduled flight of the first production Jetstream Series 31.

There was a great deal of indecision on the part of the MoD and the RAF, and several months went by whilst the relative merits of the Jetstream 31 and its rival, the Beech Super King Air, were weighed up. The RAF were said at the time to have a preference for the American-built Beech, but they were up against opposition from the Treasury. Eventually a further round of defence expenditure cuts meant that plans for a Devon/Pembroke replacement were deferred yet again. Consequently, the RAF's fleet of Devon C2s, the oldest of which, VP952, was delivered in October 1947, look set to continue in service until 1990 at least. AST 408 was formally abandoned early in 1983, when the RAF purchased four BAe HS125-700Bs. These aircraft were originally built for civil customers but

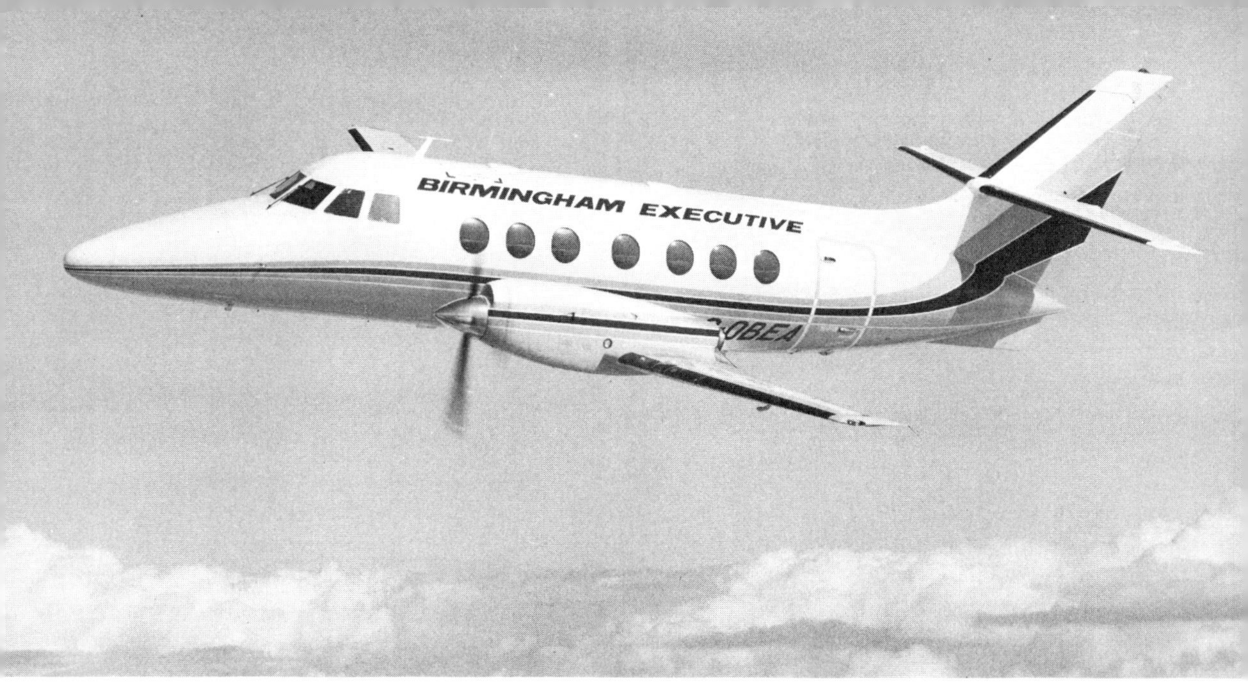

Above:
The re-engined and remodelled Jetstream 31 would have been purchased by the RAF as a Devon replacement if funds had been available in 1980-1.
British Aerospace

Below:
ZA111, previously G-AXFV, was the last military Jetstream conversion for the Royal Navy and like ZA110 could be distinguished by its blue paint scheme.
J. Guthrie

subsequently cancelled whilst still under construction. The order was later increased to six aircraft. Thus the prospect of the RAF ordering the Jetstream for the light transport/communications role has been overtaken by events yet again. It seems destined never to meet this requirement formally, although it is sometimes used by the RAF for crew ferry and provided a support 'vehicle' for the Red Arrows during the 1982 display season, when larger transport aircraft were busy elsewhere. In the training role however, the Jetstream has settled down to a long career with the RAF and the Royal Navy and apparently well past the difficulties that plagued it in the 1970s.

Fleet Air Arm Museum

F. R. Veal

Above:
HRH Prince Philip opened the original hangar of the Fleet Air Arm Museum on 28 May 1964.
Fleet Air Arm

SX137
ROYAL NAVY
SX137

ROYAL NAVY
KE 209

Left:
Supermarine Seafire XVII SX137 was one of the first aircraft to be preserved in the Museum.

Centre left:
Another of the early arrivals was this unique Hellcat II KE209, which had been flown at Lossiemouth until 1953.

Bottom left:
A line-up of the growing collection at Yeovilton in November 1968 — out of the hangar for a rare photo call.

So many motorists passing Royal Naval Air Station, Yeovilton on the busy A303 trunk road between London and the West Country stopped to watch flying that in 1963 a viewing enclosure was opened and three historic aircraft were placed nearby. The interest this created together with the celebration in 1964 of the 50th anniversary of the formation of the Royal Naval Air Service, the predecessor of today's Fleet Air Arm, led to the decision to establish a museum where historic naval aircraft and other items associated with flying in the Royal Navy could be put on public display and all kinds of records, photographs and documents could be assembled, catalogued and made available for inspection by serious students. An independent educational trust, which was granted charity status, was formed for administration with the Flag Officer Naval Air Command as Chairman of the Trustees.

The Fleet Air Arm Museum was formally opened in 1964 by HRH The Duke of Edinburgh (now the museum's patron) on the occasion of the 50th anniversary of the forma-

Below:
The start of work — 7 September 1974 saw HRH The Prince of Wales laying the foundation stone to mark the start of the Museum development project.

Right:
As well as aircraft such as this Swordfish the Museum built up an impressive array of show cases of FAA memorabilia.

Below:
This Supermarine Walrus 1 L2301 was restored at Arbroath and presented to the Museum on 6 December 1966.

tion of the Royal Naval Air Service, the predecessor of today's Fleet Air Arm.

Over the ensuing years, the museum has expanded to become one of the leading aviation museums in Europe with over 50 historic aircraft, including Concorde 002, the British-built prototype, housed under one roof in a building covering almost 100,000sq ft.

The original hangar was enlarged to today's proportions in three phases:

Phase I The Casper John Hall, linking the museum with another nearby hangar. HRH The Prince of Wales laid the foundation stone in 1974, while he was training as a helicopter pilot at Yeovilton, and the development was formally opened in 1975 by the then Prime Minister, the Rt Hon Harold Wilson.

Phase II The Queen Elizabeth Silver Jubilee Hall, which provided a workshop, library facilities, storage for archives and a lecture room, was completed in 1977 and formally opened by Admiral of the Fleet Earl Mountbatten of Burma.

Phase III Completed 1980, was named The Mountbatten Memorial Hall in Earl Mountbatten's memory, and was opened by his daughter, Countess Mountbatten.

Above:
Not all of the exhibits are complete by any means. The Short 184 8359 comprises only the forward fuselage section, being the remains that escaped wartime damage at the IWM. It is hoped that it will eventually form the basis for a reconstructed replica.

Below:
World War 2 is well covered by exhibits including the South East Asia 'Kamikaze' exhibition which opened in July 1984 and centres around the Okha II.

Above:
A special exhibition features the remains of the ex-No 800 Squadron Skua 1 L2940 which was recovered from Lake Grotli in Norway.

Below:
The Fleet Air Arm's first jets are represented by Sea Vampire 1 LZ551, which made the first jet carrier landing on 3 December 1945, and the only remaining Attacker F1, WA473.

Above right:
The Sea Fury, which performed so well in the Korean War against Mig-15 jet fighters, is featured, with WJ231 painted in the colours of an aircraft that operated from HMS Ocean.

Below right:
The period best covered is from the 1950s through to the present day, with examples of the Sea Venom, Scimitar, Buccaneer, Gannet and Sea Vixen all on display. *FAA Museum*

O

112
630

Concorde's arrival at Yeovilton for public display by the Science Museum in 1976 provided a fourth development when later housed in its own adjoining exhibition hall as an integral part of the Fleet Air Arm Museum.

An ongoing building programme has been necessary to keep pace with the continual increase in the museum's exhibits since 1964. When HRH The Duke of Edinburgh opened the first hangar, it contained just three aircraft. Four years later there were 10, and by 1973, 18, but many had to be displayed in the open.

From the arrival of Concorde in 1976, the increase in aircraft exhibits and visitors became more dramatic, and today the museum displays over 50 aircraft and receives nearly 300,000 visitors annually. In addition to the aircraft, there are many special displays, paintings, photographs, weapons, medals and uniforms, nearly 200 model aircraft and 50 superb model ships, all contributing to the story of the Royal Naval Air Service and the Fleet Air Arm.

Among the guests at the opening of the Casper John Hall in 1975 was Sir Thomas Sopwith, designer of the Sopwith Baby seaplane, a replica of which, the 'Jabberwock', now welcomes visitors to the museum in the entrance hall.

Displayed in the museum are the remains of a Short 184 comprising the engine and two cockpits, and future plans include the building of a full-sized replica of this famous aircraft, which will be exhibited with other early aircraft inside a World War 1 seaplane hangar being removed from HMS *Osprey* at Portland and re-erected alongside the museum.

In 1983 two special exhibitions were opened. The Falkland Islands Exhibition, the most comprehensive in Britain on the vital part played by the Royal Navy and its Fleet Air Arm in the campaign to retake the Falklands, was commenced immediately after hostilities ended as aircraft, equipment and relics began to be shipped to the United Kingdom. HRH The Prince Andrew who took part in the campaign, serving as a helicopter pilot in HMS *Invincible*, formally opened the exhibition on 11 July 1983.

British aircraft on display include a Wasp helicopter as used on HMS *Endurance*, and 'Humphrey', the Wessex HAS 3 helicopter from HMS *Antrim* which depth-charged the Argentinian submarine *Santa Fe,* and carried out many daring rescues on South Georgia. Its pilot, Lt Cdr Ian Stanley was awarded the DSO. 'Humphrey' is peppered with holes from cannon shrapnel while on the deck of HMS *Antrim* when she was attacked by Mirages.

The British Task Force is well represented by the many fine models of ships which served in the campaign, including HMS *Endurance* and

Below:
On 4 March 1976 the first prototype Concorde, G-BSST, was delivered to Yeovilton for permanent exhibition by the Science Museum. It has since been joined by the BAC221 and HP115 research aircraft.

Above:
The main development of the Museum and the Concorde Exhibition Hall was completed in 1980 and opened on 17 July. Buccaneer XK488 is permanently placed at the entrance.

Below:
Work on 'new' exhibits continues in the Museum. The Sea Gladiator was restored by the Society of Friends during 1982-3, visitors being able to watch the progress of the rebuild. *FAA Museum*

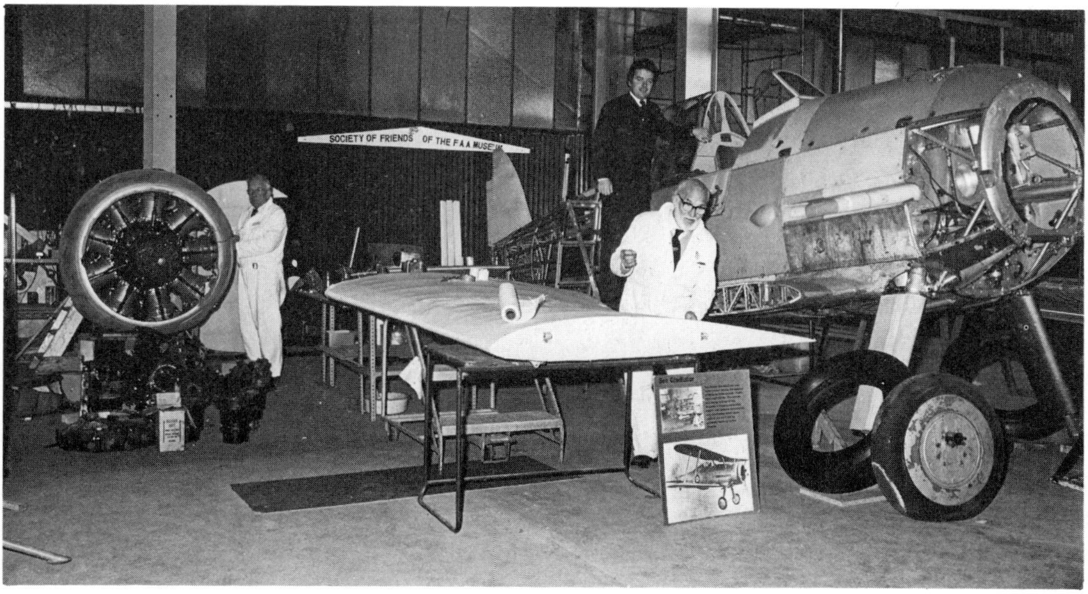

Above:
The Mountbatten Hall was transformed in 1983 to provide the most extensive record in the UK of the Falklands War. Five ex-Argentine aircraft and helicopters are on display including an air force Pucara and a navy MB339.

Above right:
Royal Navy aircraft include this Wessex HAS3, 'Humphrey', which was involved in the capture of the submarine *Sante Fe* and the rescue of Marines from crashed helicopters in appalling weather conditions.

HMS *Hermes*, and various incidents of the conflict are portrayed by dioramas and table-top models as well as through tableaux, relics, equipment, photographs and paintings.

Captured Argentinian aircraft on display include a Pucara ground-attack aircraft and the only examples of an Argentinian MB339 and Beech T-34C Turbo Mentor to be brought to Britain from the Falklands, as well as an Iroquois troop-carrying helicopter. An MB339 was responsible for bomb and rocket attacks on HMS *Argonaut* and HMS *Ardent*, which caused the latter to sink. Other Argentinian trophies displayed include a variety of equipment from small arms and rocket launchers to anti-aircraft and recoilless guns, from helmets and K-rations to a towel from the *Santa Fe.*

Wreckage from various Argentinian aircraft shot down over the Falklands is shown side-by-side with the guided missiles and rockets used in the conflict. Each item adds a paragraph to the story of the Falkland Islands campaign. Maj Juan Tomba, pilot of an Argentinian Pucara shot down by Lt Cdr 'Sharkey' Ward RN, ejected safely and presented his flying helmet to Surg-Cdr Rick Jolly RN when told by him that he could get a special tankard and tie from the British makers of the ejector seat, Martin-Baker. The helmet is displayed with part of the propeller from his Pucara.

The second exhibition opened in 1983 was a display of the remains of a Blackburn Skua which were salvaged from a depth of 90ft at the bottom of Lake Gotli in Norway in 1974 by naval divers. Royal Marine Capt R. T. Partridge leading a formation of three Skuas in 1940, encountered 25 to 30 German Heinkel bombers which were strafing an allied troop convoy. Two enemy aircraft were shot down, but Partridge's Skua was damaged and crash landed on the frozen lake. When the ice melted, the remains of the Skua sank to the bottom, where they were preserved in the fresh water until recovered 34 years later. Pieces of the Heinkel are displayed with the wrecked Skua.

In July 1984 a further special exhibition opened — the 'Kamikaze Story'. This features the Pacific Fleet in World War 2, highlighting the appearance of the Kamikaze suicide bombers, the forerunners of today's guided missiles. A Japanese Ohka rocket propelled flying bomb is displayed with a selection of British and US aircraft which took part in the Pacific War.

The Fleet Air Arm Museum is situated at RNAS Yeovilton just off the A303 road near Ilchester, Somerset. The nearest railway stations are at Yeovil (Junction and Pen Mill). Western National bus service No 478 runs between the bus station in Yeovil and the air station. The musuem is open daily except Christmas Eve and Christmas Day from 10.00 (including Bank Holidays) until 17.30 or dusk when earlier.

Admission charges include the Concorde Exhibition Hall. Special rates are offered to school and other parties on application. For further details telephone Ilchester (0935) 840565.

Roger Wright

DC-3 is 50

Without doubt one of the most famous aircraft types built must be the ubiquitous Douglas DC-3 (Douglas Commercial 3) which on the 17 December 1985 celebrates 50 years of continuous service. Little could Arthur E. Raymond, designer of the DC-3, have realised that besides becoming the most successful airliner of its time his creation would also be the most widely used military transport aircraft in the history of aviation. Evolution of the Douglas Commercial twin-engined transport aircraft began in 1932 on behalf of Trans World Airlines, for the design of an airliner to compete with the Boeing 247s of United Airlines, culminating in the test flight of the DC-1 prototype on 1 July 1933.

The production DC-2, developed directly from the DC-1 prototype, made its maiden flight on 11 May 1934, and just seven days later was pressed into service by TWA on the New York-Los Angeles route. The new airliner proved popular with the public and thus generated fierce competition betwen TWA and United Airlines, their big rival. Another competitor, American Airlines, operating Curtiss Condor bi-planes on transcontinental sleeper services found it impossible to compete with the modern Boeing 247 and Douglas DC-2 all-metal monoplanes, and so engaged on a re-equipment programme.

The DC-2 was looked on as the most favourable replacement aircraft, but American Airlines found the fuselage too narrow for the provision of sleeping berths required on their routes across the United States. Douglas was asked to produce an enlarged version of the DC-2, which ultimately resulted in the DST (Douglas Sleeper Transport). This was essentially an enlarged DC-2, consisting of the same basic structure, with a larger wing and tail surfaces and a wider fuselage. It was virtually circular in cross section, thus enabling passengers to stand upright.

The prototype DST/DC-3, which made its maiden flight at Santa Monica, Ca on 17 December 1935, had a cantilever low-wing configuration and, with the exception of fabric covered control surfaces, was of all-metal construction. The landing gear consisted of semi-retractable main wheels that retracted forwards and were located in the lower half of the engine

Above:
The start of the line. Douglas DC-1 NX223Y in TWA markings. Note the small fuselage and fin shape.
McDonnell Douglas Corp

Above:
Eastern Airlines' DC-2 photographed on 16 October 1934. *McDonnell Douglas Corp*

Below:
The first DC-3 to fly, NX14988, a Douglas Sleeper Transport, made its first flight from Clover Field, Santa Monica, Ca on 17 December 1935.
McDonnell Douglas Corp

nacelles, and a fully retractable castoring tail wheel. Pneumatic de-icing boots were provided on the leading edges of the wings, fin and tailplanes and was powered by 920hp Wright Cyclone engines. Pratt & Whitney 1,000hp R-1380 Twin-Wasps were offered as an alternative shortly afterwards. American Airlines took delivery of the new aircraft in two versions; the DST with 16 sleeping berths and the 24 seater DC-3. Following type certification on 21 May 1938 the airline commenced nonstop flights between New York-Chicago with the DST on 25 June 1936.

Strategists of the United States Army Air Force (USAAF) were increasingly attracted to the DC-3, realising its suitability for a variety of military roles. This resulted in Douglas Aircraft being issued with a directive for design modifications that included a reinforced cabin floor and fuselage strengthening aft of the wing root to allow for double cargo doors each 4ft 6in wide to be fitted. The Douglas design team had already envisaged the military aspects and a basic design was already complete for a C-41 cargo prototype that was powered by two 1,200hp Pratt & Whitney Twin-Wasps in a DC-2 conversion. Evaluation was carried out by the US Army and the delivery of a militarised DC-3 in October 1938 proved to be

Above and left:
The C-47 made a major contribution to the D-Day invasion of Normandy in June 1944. Here USAAF and RAF Dakotas are lined up at RAF Greenham Common, Berks prior to the landings.
Roger Wright Collection

the vanguard of more than 10,000 military versions to be built. An initial production order for 545 military DC-3s, given the military designation C-47 Skytrain was issued to Douglas on 18 September 1940. Douglas had already experienced considerable success, with 430 DC-1 to 3 variants having entered airline service by this time, including 18 purchased by the Russian airline Aeroflot in 1937, designated PS-84s.

World War 2 had already commenced and demand by the RAF for aircraft from US manufacturers was desperate, the C-47 being included in the shopping list. Aircraft production capacity was taken over by the US Military Services, coinciding with an extension of the initial USAAF order for C-47s from 545 to 953. This included 30 aircraft for the RAF which were designated Dakota Is. With production capacity fully utilised at Santa Monica Douglas opened up a new facility at Long Beach, Ca to build the C-47. The USAAF began acceptance of the Skytrain in January 1941 and by November of that year and America's entry into the war, over 500 had already been constructed and pressed into service. A shortage was still apparent, which resulted in the requisition and conversion of prewar DC-3s in US Airline service for military use.

The new Long Beach plant could not meet the growing production requirements for the USAAF and RAF so a second line was opened up at Tulsa, Oklahoma. The first model constructed here was the new 24V system C-47A, which replaced the original C-47 with its inadequate 12V electrical system; 962 of these aircraft entered service with the RAF as Dakota IIIs. The second production variant was the C-47B which had larger engines with two-stage superchargers as one of its modifications for operations in hot and high conditions. This type was used extensively throughout China and Burma; the RAF having 896 of the mark designated Dakota IV.

Below:
Postwar airlines like Aer Lingus bought up the surplus C-47s to provide the mainstay on European routes for more than 10 years.

Bottom:
Similarly in the UK the independent airlines such as Cambrian Airways made extensive use of Dakotas for their domestic and cross-Channel services.

The C-53 Skytrooper variant was built in relatively small numbers as a basic 28-man parachute platform glider tug. Unlike the C-47 it did not have the cargo doors and reinforced floor and was very similar to the original DC-3 design. The C-53 was to prove the concept for the glider-tug C-47. Following field development trials, towing cleats were subsequently fitted to all C-47 types. The important part to be played by the 'para-dropping' C-47 quickly became apparent with the dropping of 3,900 paratroops during the invasion of Sicily in July 1943. The countless missions flown to provide support for Brigadier Wingates' Chindits in Burma during the preceding winter of 1942 had already proved its value as an air supply and support aircraft.

The reliability and suitably of the C-47 for the paradropping/glider tug role was long taken for

Top:
After the war Douglas C-47s and variants remained in service with many of the world's air forces including the USAF. It came into its own again during the early part of the Vietnam war.

Above:
The 'Super-Skytrain' saw service particularly with the US Navy. Note the modified fin and rudder and undercarriage doors.

granted in the numerous war offensive planning centres. 1944 was to see the 'coming of the age' for the C-47. During the initial stages of the D-Day invasions which commenced on 6 June 1944, 1,100 Allied C-47s positioned 25,000 men and machines attached to the British 6th and American 82nd and 101st Airborne Divisions. Records showed that during the 72 hours of the operation C-47s disgorged almost 65,000 paratroopers in the largest aerial assault ever launched.

With the defeat of Hitler's Reich in May 1945, followed by capitulation of the Japanese Empire on 15 August 1945, further production of the C-47/DC-3 was terminated and the orders for 1,405 C-47Bs and 114 C-117As, a military VIP version of the C-47 were cancelled. Military production ceased with 10,048 C-47s having being built in just over four years.

A variety of designated types of the C-47 emerged during the wartime period of construction, many to meet special operating requirements. In addition to the A and B types that

Above:
The pilot's office of Dakota G-AMSV is relatively simple by comparison with the modern jet-liner. *Roger Wright*

equipped the USAAF and RAF, 680 were commissioned into US Navy and Marine service in a variety of designations that comprised the R4D-1 (C-47), R4D-3 (C-53), R4D-4 (C-53C), R4D-5 (C-47A), R4D-6 (C-47B) and R4D-7 (TC-47B) together with conversions which included the electronics equipped R4D-5E/6E, radar countermeasures R4D-4Q/5Q/6Q, air-sea warfare training R4D-5S/6S and VIP equipped R4D-5Z/6Z, the Navy and Marine VIP equivalent of the USAAF C-117A and B. During the period of wartime production of the C-47/DC-3, it is worth noting that although 24 variants of Wright Cyclone and Pratt & Whitney Twin Wasp engines were developed, the basic airframe design was employed basically unchanged throughout, thus proving the quality of the original design.

During WW2 the C-47, in all its variants, was operational in every Allied war zone and with the end of hostilities thousands of these Douglas transport aircraft became available for civil use overnight at 'knock-down' prices. Figures quoted of £2,500 for an airworthy DC-3 complete with spares were no exception. Many of the type were given quick and cheap internal conversions and with the addition of seats became the workhorse of the airline industry for the next 15 years. It is fair to state that 90% of major airline operators of the postwar period had at least one DC-3 on their inventory.

Exactly four years after the D-Day invasion of 1944 the Soviet Forces enforced the blockade of Berlin. What followed was the largest airlift of food and coal imaginable, totalling some 2,443,315 tons. 470 C-47/DC-3s participated in the massive operation amongst the many transport types employed to fly into the beleagured city round the clock.

On 17 April 1961 a USAF C-47D equipped with a variety of sensors and cameras was shot down by Communist forces deep inside Laos while seeking out North Vietnamese dispositions. This was the first military aircraft to be lost by the US armed forces in the escalating war between North and South Vietnam. Thus the C-47 was back at war. French forces had successfully operated some 70 C-47s as transports and para-droppers during their involvement in the initial years of hostility, as

indeed the South Vietnamese Air Force had likewise. However, the 'Gooney Bird' nicknamed by the Military Air Command of the USAF was merely a stand-by hack and was never seriously considered for transport duties in this theatre.

Specialised variants of the C-47 were extensively used however. The EC-47D, for example, patrolled the borders and coastlines of North Vietnam collating enemy radio signals and intelligence-gathering with great effect. By means of triangulation the interpreters were able to determine locations for the massive strikes by B-52 bombers. RC-47s of the South Vietnamese AF were used in the location and observation of munition movements from North Vietnam

Above:
In the 1980s, Jersey based Air Atlantique has been the largest operator of Dakotas in the British Isles, using them for postal, freight and passenger charter operations.

Below:
Dakotas still have diverse uses. This aircraft, G-AMPZ, is operated by Harvestair under contract to the Department of Transport for pollution control duties.

southwards, both overland along the Yo Chi Minh Trail and by sea in junks. The low speed of the C-47 proved valuable as it was found that the high-speed jets summoned to the aid of ground forces under night attack had difficulty in locating the Viet Cong, who depended on darkness and jungle rather than anti-aircraft weapons for defence: the answer was a low-speed aircraft that could fly at night, locate the enemy and direct accurate fire power against them. Capt Ronald Terry recalled how missionaries in Latin America delivered supplies with baskets suspended from a tightly circling airplane. He noted that the basket remained within a small area and wondered if the same principle could be applied to automatic weapons firing air-to-ground; the result being 'Puff the Magic Dragon', the C-47 gunship.

AC-47D gunship was the official designation of this 'new' variant which carried three multi-barrel 7.62mm machine guns with a fire-power of 18,000 rounds/min located in two window apertures and the door, along with flare dispensers for night target illumination. The success of the concept was devastating as far as the enemy was concerned and resulted in the formation of two squadrons of AC-47D's called 'Spookies'; the effectiveness of which resulted in the development of the AC-130 gunship.

Production of the DC-3 also took place under licence. Russia built an estimated 2,700 aircraft designated Li-2. These could be distinguished as they were fitted with the passenger door on the starboard side of the fuselage. A total of 707 C-47s were also supplied to the Soviet Union through the Lend-Lease programme and given the NATO code-name 'Cab'; it is believed a number of the type are still in use within the Eastern bloc. A further 576 examples were constructed in Japan by Showa and Nakajima designated L2D and reports suggest that over 1,000 aircraft with an exact resemblance to the DC-3 have been built in China.

In civilian use the Douglas DC-3 has played a significant part in establishing new routes and airlines throughout the world; the type still proving popular in South America. In this, its 50th year of operation, estimates quote some 480 still remaining in civilian use with a further 1,100 on active service in military configurations. The oldest known example, still flying, is operated by PBA (Province Town, Boston Airlines) registered N136PB. 'Old Thirty Six' as the aircraft is nick-named, breaks a record every time it gets airborne. The DC-3, which first entered service with Eastern Airlines as NC18121 on 25 October 1937, flies on average 2,000 hours each year and to date has flown a total of 88,000 hours ($10\frac{1}{2}$ years in the air). An older example which might yet fly again belongs to the Science Museum's transport collection and is located at Wroughton, Wiltshire. This DC-3 registered EI-AYO first entered service with United Airlines in 1937 as NC16071. Plans are afoot to restore and repaint the aircraft to carry United's markings of that period.

Who would have thought in those early days of commercial aviation that in 50 years' time a direct successor to the DC-3 that is superior in comfort, economy and reliability, would not be found. Arthur Raymond, aircraft designer of yesteryear certainly didn't. You can be sure no designer of today could possibly admit to having yet found a replacement for the world's most successful airliner. With its basic and robust construction having taken all that can be inflicted upon it, you can be sure that a DC-3 will still be airborne on its 75th anniversary — but that's another story.

Right:
The second oldest surviving Dakota in the world, EI-AYO was the 24th off the line in 1936 as NC16071 for United Airlines. It is now preserved by the Science Museum at Wroughton.